The Cook is the Captain

The Cook is the Captain

Neil Hollander and Harald Mertes

Graphics by Putty Koehler

W · W · Norton & Company · Inc · New York

First American Edition 1979

ISBN 0-393-03234-5

Printed in Great Britain

Dedication

To Martha, Sabina, Heloisa, Margarita, Chantal, Christa, Nadia, Irmela, Maggie, Melody, Viviane and Yvonne who saved us from starvation by taking over the cooking while we were writing this book.

Acknowledgments

We are grateful to the authors, publishers and literary agents for permission to use quotations in the text of this book, from: *The Old Man and the Sea* by Ernest Hemingway – the Executors of the Ernest Hemingway Estate; Jonathan Cape Ltd, London; Charles Scribner's Sons, New York. *Mr Midshipman Hornblower* by C. S. Forester – Michael Joseph, London, reprinted by permission of A. D. Peters & Co. Ltd., *Trimaran Solo* by Nigel Tetley – The Nautical Publishing Co. Ltd. *The Long Way* by Bernard Moitessier – Adlard Coles Ltd./Granada Publishing Ltd.; translated from 'La Longue Route' – Editions Arthaud, Grenoble; published in the USA by Doubleday & Co. Inc. *Kon-Tiki Expedition* by Thor Heyerdahl (1950) – George Allen & Unwin Publishers Ltd.; published in the USA by Rand McNally & Co. *The Impossible Voyage* by Chay Blyth – Hodder & Stoughton Ltd. *The Last Grain Race* by Eric Newby – George Allen & Unwin Ltd. *Sea Wolf and Selected Stories* by Jack London – Signet Books Ltd. *The Ship Captain's Medical Guide* – Department of Trade and Industry (HMSO). *The Guinness Book of Records* – Guinness Superlatives Ltd, Publishers. *The Bombard Story* translated from the French 'Naufrage Solitaire' – Editions de Paris – by Brian Connell – Andre Deutsch Ltd. *117 Days Adrift* by Maurice and Maralyn Bailey – The Nautical Publishing Co. Ltd, 1973; published as 'Staying Alive' in USA and Canada – David McKay Co. Inc, New York. *Survive the Savage Sea* by Dougal Robertson – Paul Elek Ltd. 1973.

The Illustration on page 132 is from the MGM release *Ship From Shanghai* *c* 1930 Metro-Goldwyn Mayer Distributing Corporation. Copyright renewed by Loew's Incorporated in 1957. The 'Moby Dick' graphics are from illustrations by Rockwell Kent, published by Random House.

NH and HM

Contents

'Of all the books produced since the most remote ages by human talents and industry those only that treat of cooking are, from a moral point of view, above suspicion. The intention of every other piece of prose may be discussed and even mistrusted; but the purpose of a cookery book is one and unmistakable. Its object can conceivably be no other than to increase the happiness of mankind.'

Joseph Conrad, Preface to A Handbook of Cookery

Who is the Captain?

For centuries the notion has persisted that the Captain is in charge of his ship. But this is merely a myth, a thin façade of law and custom. The Cook is the Captain, and he always has been.

True, the Captain presents himself as the all-powerful commander who armed with his sextant, tables and telescope assumes responsibility for the ship's course. But with modern technology navigation is hardly a skill. To move from point A to point B today's Captain simply sets the auto-pilot or wind vane then lazily stares at the sea dreaming about the days when he had something important to do.

Meanwhile, the Cook labours in his galley, creating not just the next meal, but that special, light-hearted spirit which is so vital to any voyage. For some traditions never die. As always, food at sea is the sailor's strength, his tonic and his joy. And no one knows this better than the Cook. He is the caretaker of the crew's mood, the ship's guardian, mediator and confessor.

Unlike the Captain, who maintains his customary distance, the Cook is intimately involved with all that happens on board. Conflicts, secrets, triumphs, complaints and gossip all pass across his galley table. He knows everyone's likes and dislikes, their foibles, passions and sensitivities. More than anyone else, he is in tune with the pulse of the crew. Delicately balancing the needs of the love-sick, home-sick, land-sick and sea-sick, the Cook constructs his menus as though he were trimming the ship.

During a long passage when days are quiet and boredom silently creeps on board, the smell of cakes, soufflés and chowder rakes the ship, drawing everyone to the galley. With pride and purpose, the Cook welds his crew together. Over platters of steaming delicacies, arguments dissolve and friendship is kindled.

Should a crisis strike – a sudden onshore wind, a fouled anchor or a raging gale – the Cook knows just how much rum to put in each man's grog, and when the Captain's composure begins to crack, the Cook hurries to his side with a well-laced mug of coffee and a few words of encouragement.

Wherever the ship ventures – calm waters or troubled seas – the Cook is always on duty, diligently nourishing his crew. Usually somewhere in the background, his uniform never adorned with rank or decoration, he is unsung in song, verse or prose. But as every sailor knows, *The Cook is the Captain.*

A Note on the Recipes

The recipes in this book were collected during a three-year voyage which took us from the Mediterranean to the Atlantic, the Caribbean and finally the South Pacific. Wherever possible, we looked over the shoulders of chefs on board freighters, liners and charter boats, poked our noses into harbour kitchens, and interviewed the Cooks of fishing boats and cruising yachts. And every Cook we spoke to agreed: *the Cook is the Captain.*

In spite of this, as everyone knows, Captains still exist, and virtually every boat afloat, from a dinghy to a liner, has one. Usually, it is readily apparent who he is. He's the man who screams the loudest, gestures the wildest, has the worst vocabulary and, of course, does the least work.

However, with us, spectators were never really sure. Often, they would ask, 'Who is the skipper?'

Our answer was always: 'We're two Cooks without a Captain.'

Strange as that may sound, it's quite true. Besides eating better than most yachts, we've found our system, or lack of it, to be a much easier way to sail. Without a Captain, we've had no problems with discipline, dissension and despotism – the latter being a rather common disease among Captains. This is not to say that our boat has not been without its conflicts. Just as it is an intolerable situation to have two Captains on board, it is equally difficult to have two Cooks. The question arises: Who is chief Cook?

To avoid this problem, we rotate every day. And that, by the way, is a luxury Captains cannot afford. Each day one of us has the privilege of being the Cook, while the other must suffer with the boring mechanical tasks of navigation and boat handling.

The Cook for the day posts his menu on the bulkhead the night before – three meals, bread, tea, evening grog and midnight snack. The next morning he takes complete charge of the galley. All preparation, serving and washing up are his responsibility. And as an incentive to better cuisine, we developed the rule: If the Cook on duty can successfully produce a completely new dish, and find an appropriate name for it, then as a reward he can remain Cook for another day.

Perhaps this sounds a bit unorthodox for a cruising yacht, but we can only say that it has worked for us across two oceans. Instead of wasting our time splicing, varnishing, sewing sails and scouring the bilge, we have stimulated our creative talents and thoroughly enjoyed every meal of the voyage.

For this reason many of the recipes in this book are of our own invention.

For example, during the first week of July 1976 we were becalmed at 12° 42′ S.–110° 15′ W., that is, right in the middle of the Pacific. According to our log, the day's menu listed pizza Napolitana for lunch. However, we had a large number of flying fish in the galley left over from breakfast.

We managed to spend the morning discussing the possibilities: Should we use the fish as bait, put them in a marinade, make fishburgers or a curry, or a soup? Finally, as lunchtime approached the obvious became obvious and pizza Napolitana was transformed into Flying Fish Pizza (page 124).

That, we think, was one of our best creations. It was so good in fact that we had it for lunch or dinner nearly every day until we ran out of oregano.

Several weeks later while we were at anchor in the lagoon of Fakarawa we found ourselves with about 75 kilos of shark hanging from the main halyard.

Normally we have an unspoken agreement with sharks – if they'll leave us alone, we'll do the same. But this shark broke the contract.

We had been fishing over the side and every time we hooked a fish, a black shadow would appear from underneath the boat and instantly fish and tackle were lost. It was clear that if we wanted lunch we would have to dispose of the shark first. Apparently, he was as hungry as we were, for when we dropped a large hook baited with a fish head in the water, he pounced on it immediately. Then we slowly winched him on board.

We had heard from other cruising people that shark meat tends to be tough and rubbery and that the only valuable part are the jaws which can be sold to tourists, but we decided to experiment anyway. We cut fillets from different parts of the shark and spent the afternoon making stews, curries and soups. Our best recipe turned out to be marinated Shark Steaks taken from near the tail (page 124).

Harbours have always been a great source of recipes and nearly every port we visited filled a few pages of our galley book.

An old single-hander we met in Port-of-Spain, whose boat, dog and name were 'Rummy' and who used rum in almost everything he cooked, was delighted to give us the formula for some of his favourite dishes: Rum and Bananas (page 112), Rum Carrots (page 115), Cannon Rum Balls (page 101), and Poseidon's Rum Pancakes (page 84). In Bahia, Brazil, the Cook of a German freighter who invited himself on board after smelling our Ratatouille (page 44) taught us how to make Kartoffelpuffer (page 60), the famous German potato pancakes, and also gave us the recipes for Bauernfrühstück (page 68), Cabbage Salad (page 25), and Beer Soup (page 41). Further south at la Boca in Buenos Aires we persuaded a retired sea-cook, the owner of a portside restaurant, to part with his special version of the Argentine steak sauce, Chimischurri (page 94).

Occasionally people have offered us recipes, and in one instance at a very timely moment.

While we were alongside the quay in Port Vendre preparing for the voyage, early one morning a fork-lift carrying trays of fresh anchovies raced down the dock. Just as it passed us one wheel bounced into a pothole, the load balanced precariously for a second or two, then an avalanche of anchovies tumbled on to our deck.

'What are you going to do about all these fish?' we asked the driver.

'That's your problem now,' he replied and drove off.

We fried some of the anchovies for lunch, and gave away as many as we could to the other yachts in the harbour; but we still had enough left to start a cannery. Finally a fisherman showed us how to salt them in buckets using an old method which he claimed would preserve them for months.

He was right. We ate the last anchovy nearly three months later off the Cap Verde Islands (Anchovies in a Bucket – page 21).

Fishermen taught us a great deal, and whenever we had the chance we would spend a day or two working on their boats. In Spain we fished for sardines, in Brazil for dorados and in the

Caribbean for tuna. We learned not only how to improve our own catch, but how to make simple one-pot meals and, more importantly, how to mix a warming, potent grog (Chapter 14).

During a couple of lazy months in the Touamotous and Society Islands we often went fishing with the natives. Very quickly we found ourselves becoming integrated into Polynesian life. Nearly by habit we would string the fish on fronds, share the catch with the village and eat it raw à la Tahitienne (page 123).

Why we left the islands we really don't know.

However, we did come back to Europe, turned our backs to the sea and sifted through our notebooks and experiences. The result is this book.

The recipes are designed for small boat galleys, without refrigeration or electrics, but with a two-burner stove. An oven, although certainly convenient, is not essential since it can usually be improvised (page 9); whenever one is required, the oven symbol appears beside the recipe.

As baking temperature is often difficult to judge and maintain, especially when a boat is at sea, we have indicated simply a 'warm', 'moderate' or 'hot' oven.

The number of portions recipes serve varies from chapter to chapter since the book is organized according to situations a Cook must cope with, for example, a boat full of landlubbers, a mermaid aboard for dinner or a thirsty crew ready for a celebration.

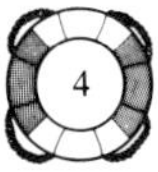

A number inside the liferaft symbol indicates approximately how many portions the recipe will make. And should that prove to be too many or too few we have tried to simplify proportions so they can easily be halved or doubled.

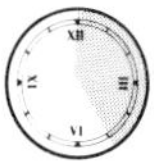

The preparation time for a dish depends on a number of factors – skill, organization of the galley, help or hindrance from the crew, distractions, etc. – none the less, we have placed a clock beside each recipe with a 'guesstimate'. This does not include any standing, rising or marinating time.

We have also attempted to keep units of measurement simple, using whenever possible pinches, palmfuls and fingers. A pinch is roughly a quarter of a teaspoon, a palmful about two well-rounded tablespoons and a finger of liquor is one shot in a water glass the thickness of any finger except the thumb.

Although we have used the conventional cup measurement for

ingredients such as sugar and flour, an empty soup tin can easily be substituted. Cups can also be measured by the handful. Most Cooks we spoke to used this method, and after a little practice we also developed the habit.

Another habit we acquired was writing down our culinary experiences. Just as any Captain likes to show off his logbook, we'd like to present some recipes from our galley-book. For some sailors an entry like 'Wind Force 10, sleet, hail and mountainous seas . . .' may bring back fond memories, but for us a far more pleasant recollection comes when we read '. . . cut in thin slices, marinate in rum and flambé . . .'

Glossary of Terms and Measurements

	UK	USA	Metric
Cans			approx.
small	5 ounces	5 ounces	140 grams
medium	13$\frac{1}{2}$ ounces	13$\frac{1}{2}$ ounces	380 grams
large	1 pound 3 ounces	1 pound 3 ounces	540 grams
Cups (liquid)	8 fluid ounces	1 cup	250 ml
Cups (solids)			
Cheese (grated)	$\frac{1}{4}$ pound	1 cup	125 grams
Flour	$\frac{1}{4}$ pound	1 cup	125 grams
Sugar: white	$\frac{1}{2}$ pound	1 cup	250 grams
brown	7 ounces	1 cup	210 grams
icing	4$\frac{1}{2}$ ounces	1 cup	140 grams
Quart	32 fluid ounces	1 quart	1 litre
Tablespoon	$\frac{1}{2}$ ounce	$\frac{1}{2}$ ounce	15 grams
Butter	$\frac{1}{4}$ pound	stick	125 grams
Yeast	1 ounce dry	1 packet	30 grams

Galley Implements

Mortar and pestle

The old way is still best: grinding spices, making powders, even crushing garlic

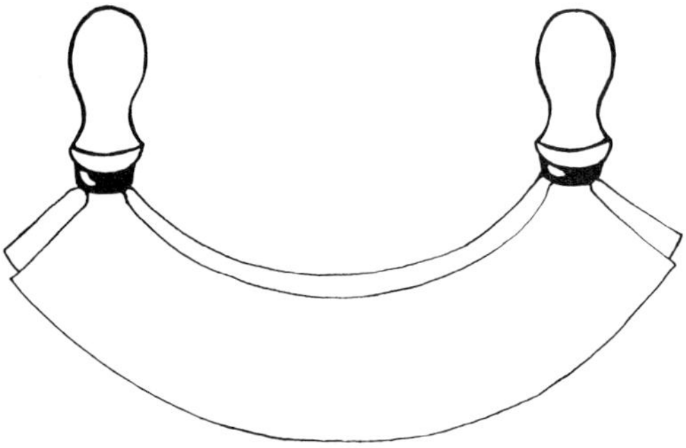

Chopper

Dicing and chopping are easier done with two hands than one

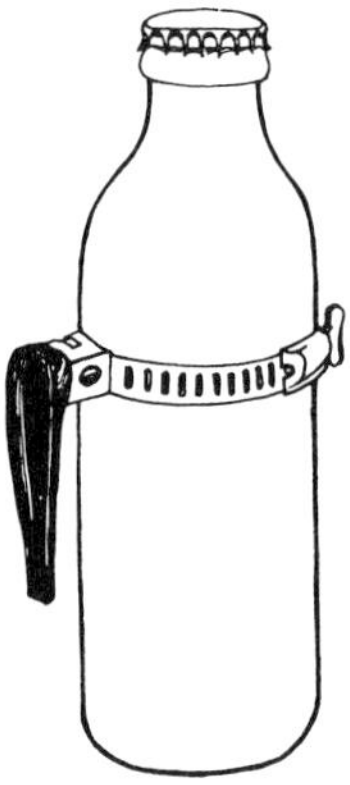

Bottle handle

Handles on bottles of cooking oil, vinegar and liquid soap make a big difference when the sea is rough

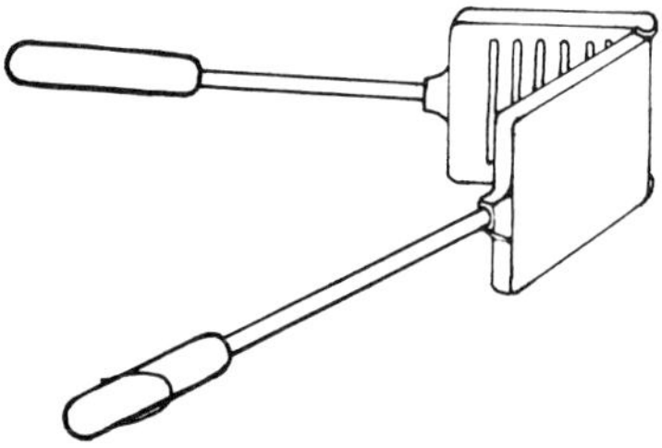

Sandwich grill

Almost any sandwich is tastier toasted

Tea board

A simple way to serve four cups of tea and still have one hand for the boat

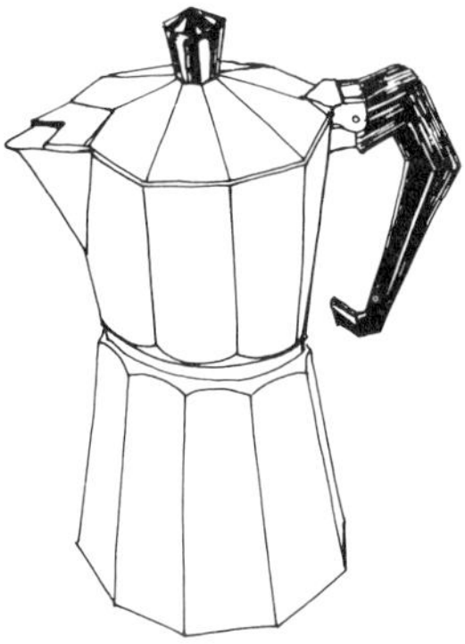

Coffee maker

Expresso for the dog-watch

How to make an Oven

Even the simplest Primus stove can be transformed into an oven so that the Cook can turn out bread, cakes, casseroles and baked fish.

Here are two methods we have used successfully:

1 Put a wire grill, or an inverted aluminium pie tin with holes cut in its side, in the bottom of a Dutch oven to form a rack on which the baking dish is placed. In this way heat will circulate around the dish. Be sure to keep the flame low so as not to scorch the bottom.

2 Cut a door in a side of a large biscuit tin and drill 3 or 4 holes in each of the adjacent sides. Thread a long bolt or screw through each of them. Then lay a thin sheet of aluminium over them, or attach a wire grill. Place the open end of the tin over the burner.

The Larder's Lifespan

Milk and cream	1–2 days	Store in original containers
Cheese		
Hard, blue and cheddar	More than a week	Re-wrap in aluminium foil
Butter		
Unsalted	1 week	Store in original containers
Salted	Several weeks	
Margarine	Nearly in-definitely	
Eggs		
Raw	1 week	See insert 'Eggs for the Voyage', page 130
Boiled	2 days	
Prepared	Up to 4 months	
Meat		
Raw	1–2 days	Wrap in oil coated paper so the meat does not become hard and stiff
Boiled	1–2 days	
Salted	6 months	
Dried	6 months	
Fish		
Raw	1 day	See insert 'Fresh Fish', page 38
Cooked	less than 1 day	
Shellfish	less than 1 day	
Poultry	1 day	

Vegetables		
Green	2 days	Store in a basket in a dark, well ventilated place
Others	Minimum 1 week	
Fruits	In general, 2 weeks	Those with hard skins should be stored in nets, with soft skins, wrapped and packed in boxes

Basic Spices

Basil: tomato, fish, cheese and egg dishes; stews, soups

Bay leaves: soup stocks, stews, casseroles

Cayenne: sauces, chillis, egg and shellfish dishes

Cinnamon: *sticks:* coffee, teas, mulled wine; *ground:* puddings, cakes, stewed fruits

Cloves: *whole:* mulled wines, stewed fruits, ham, barbecued meat; *ground:* cakes, buns, puddings

Oregano: pizza, sauces, salad dressings, grilled meat

Paprika: cream sauces, crabmeat, chicken and cheese dishes

Pepper: *whole:* soups, stews, pickles, boiled meat

Rosemary: lamb, veal, pork

Sage: *leaves:* tea; *ground:* cold meat – particularly lamb – grilled pork, chicken, salad dressings

Tarragon: soups, salad dressings, fish and shellfish dishes

Thyme: meat dishes, soups, stuffings, mushrooms, aubergines

Notes on Water

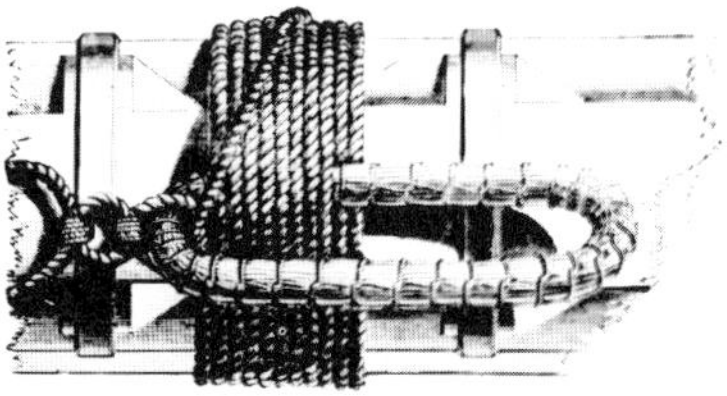

Salt-water Cooking

Fresh water at sea is always in short supply. Without ill effects or loss of taste, rice, potatoes and pasta can be cooked in salt water. However, the potatoes should be unpeeled, and the pasta and rice will be more glutinous than normal. Diluted with fresh water, sea water can also be used in bread and biscuit making and to cook raw vegetables.

Keeping Fresh Water Fresh

There are now products on the market which will clean and disinfect the tubes, tanks and connections of the water system and purify the water as well. Many of these products work without the use of chlorine, hence they are not dangerous and will not alter the water's taste or smell. They are usually found in tablets or powder; about 2–5 grams per 100 litres is sufficient.

Catching Rainwater

Traditionally, sailors have hung a bucket on the boom and collected rainwater as it ran off the sail. But the first few buckets were always salty and useless. To make the most of any squall, we used a plastic sheet with lengths of cord attached to the corners and sides. Depending upon the direction of the wind, we tied the sheet between the shrouds and the mast or boom. Pure rainwater poured into our jerrycans.

Cooling Water on the Open Sea

On a long cruise or a hot day at anchor it's a refreshing luxury to have a cool drink – tea, lemonade or juice. In the Tropics sailors have traditionally poured their tea into bottles, wrapped them in wet rags or sail cloth and hauled them aloft. As every schoolboy knows, the drying effect of the wind cools the liquid in the bottle. We found this method so useful that an old wine bottle wrapped in burlap was a permanent part of our rigging.

Chapter 1

The Old Salt

'But I made it up by eating some salt beef and biscuit, which I found to be the invariable accompaniment of every meal; the sailors sitting cross-legged on their chests in a circle, and breaking the hard biscuit, very sociably, over each other's heads, which was very convenient indeed, but gave me the headache, at least for the first four or five days till I got used to it; and then I did not care much about, only it kept my hair full of crumbs; and I had forgot to bring a fine comb and brush, so I used to shake my hair out to windward over the bulwarks every morning.'

Herman Melville, Redburn

You sit in the cockpit ready to cast off. Finally, your crew comes walking up the dock. It will be his first time at sea, and his new oilskins squeak loudly with every step. Slung over his shoulder is a dufflebag, undoubtedly full of useless gear, and in his mind are dreams of clipper ships and stout-hearted men. Although it's just a weekend cruise, he's expecting the Horn, and ready to be thrust before, behind or on top of the mast.

You dash below and hide your fine patés, sauces and spices. Cakes and sweets, scotch and cognac, Wedgwood china and linens also go into the locker. On the galley table you place a battered tin plate and a wooden spoon, and on the stove, a single, worn pot.

Why destroy his dream, when you can nourish it with hard tack, grog and bubble and squeak.

Hard Tack

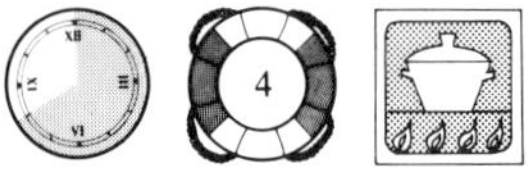

1 pound flour
½ teaspoon salt water

Mix salt and flour, then add water slowly until dough is stiff. Roll on a floured board, making a crust about a half inch thick. Cut into squares or rounds with a cookie cutter or an opened tin can, prick surface with a fork and bake in a hot oven until golden brown. When stored in a dry place, hard tack will keep indefinitely.

Boston Brown Bread

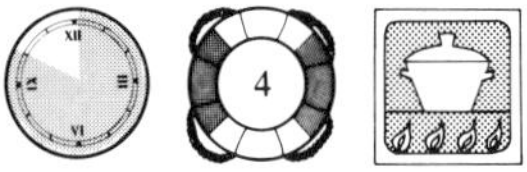

1 cup flour
1 cup cornmeal
1 cup whole wheat flour
1 teaspoon salt
1 teaspoon baking soda
1 teaspoon baking powder
2 cups of buttermilk
¾ cup molasses
chopped raisins or nuts

Mix all the dry ingredients together, then slowly stir in the molasses and milk. Beat well. Traditionally, Boston Brown Bread is cooked in small round loaves which are steamed in a Dutch oven for 2–3 hours. Empty vegetable cans make perfect baking pans. The dough may also be poured into a normal sized pan and baked in a moderate oven for 30–45 minutes.

Spiced Pickled Eggs

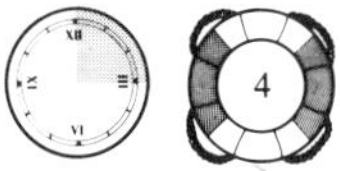

8 hard-boiled eggs
1 onion, sliced
½ cup vinegar
½ cup sugar
½ cup water
1 garlic clove, crushed
pinch of dill
pinch of allspice
pinch of salt

Put eggs in a glass jar and cover them with onions. Then heat the water, sugar, vinegar and spices in a pot and let boil for several minutes. Pour over the eggs, cover and set aside for 2–3 days before serving.

Sunday Dinner

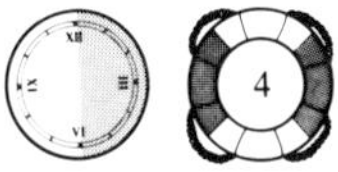

1 large can of corned beef
4 medium-sized potatoes
1 onion, chopped
2 green peppers, chopped
1 small can of tomato (sauce) juice
4 eggs
2 tablespoons cooking oil
salt and pepper

Peel, boil and mash the potatoes, then set them to one side. Cut the meat into small chunks and cook it with the green peppers and onions in the tomato sauce. When the vegetables are soft, add the mashed potatoes, and mix well. In a separate pan, fry the eggs in oil, and serve on top of each portion of meat and potatoes.

Grand Banks Baked Beans

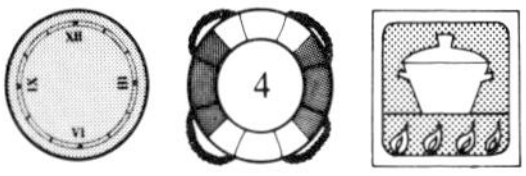

2 large cans baked beans
5 rashers (slices) bacon
1 small onion, chopped
2 tablespoons brown sugar
dash of Worcester sauce
pinch of dry mustard
pinch of pepper

Fry the bacon until crisp and remove from pan. Cook onions, adding crumbled bacon, sugar, Worcester sauce and beans. Season with mustard and pepper. Place in a covered casserole, and bake for at least one hour in a moderate oven.

Pickled Onions

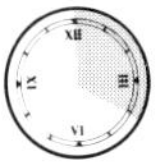
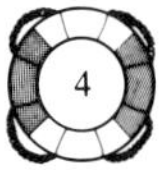

2 pounds of small onions
2 tablespoons salt
2 cups white vinegar
½ cup (6 tablespoons) sugar
½ teaspoon dill
1 teaspoon mixed pickle spice

Boil onions for three minutes, remove skins and ends, then place in a jar. Cover with water and salt and let stand overnight. Then drain liquid. In a small pot heat vinegar, sugar, dill and pickle spice until it boils, then pour over the onions. Seal and store.

A Poor Sailor's Lunch

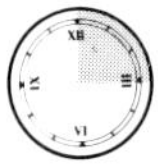
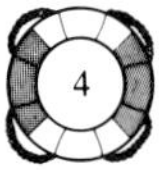

10 slices of stale bread
3 eggs
4 tablespoons sugar
1 cup milk
3 tablespoons breadcrumbs
⅓ stick (1½ oz) of butter or margarine
pinch of cinnamon

Mix the eggs, milk and 2 tablespoons of sugar. Dip the bread, slice by slice, but don't let it soak. Cover both sides with bread-crumbs and fry in butter until brown Mix cinnamon and rest of sugar and sprinkle on before serving.

Bubble and Squeak

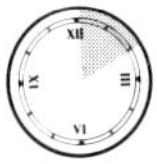

cooked potatoes
cooked cabbage
salt and pepper
lard

Potatoes and cabbages are sliced and in equal proportions placed in a frying pan. Traditionally, lard, and plenty of it, is used, but oil or margarine improves the taste. Cook until crisp and brown.

Onion and Potato Soup

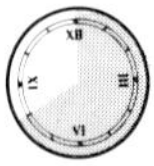
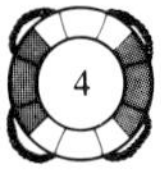

2–3 potatoes, peeled and diced
2 onions, chopped
3 cups of chicken broth
½ cup of milk
2 tablespoons butter or margarine
salt and pepper

Melt butter in a large casserole, then add potatoes, onions and broth. Simmer for at least half an hour, stirring occasionally to break up the potatoes. Season with salt and pepper. Add milk and serve, hot or cold.

Deadeye Soup

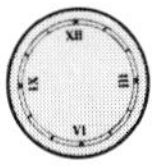
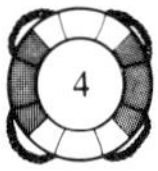

1 cup dried lentils
1 ham bone or chunks of salt pork
2 quarts of beef bouillon
1 onion, minced
2 potatoes, diced
¼ stick (1 oz) of butter or margarine
1–2 bay leaves
2 cloves of garlic, crushed

Soak the lentils in water for several hours, then heat them till they come to the boil. Remove from the stove and drain off the liquid. Add the bouillon, ham bone, bay leaves, onion and garlic. Boil the soup, then simmer for several hours. The longer, the better. Half an hour before serving, add potatoes and butter. Season to taste and remove the bone.

Stale-Bread Omelette

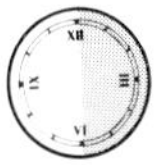
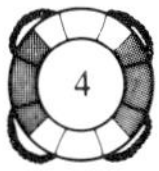

10–12 slices of stale bread
1 cup milk
3–4 eggs
2 tablespoons sugar
2 tablespoons butter or margarine

Cut the bread into small pieces and place in a casserole. In a bowl, mix the eggs, milk and sugar, then pour over the bread and let stand for about 20 minutes. Heat butter in a frying pan, add bread mixture and cook like an omelette.

Fish Chowder

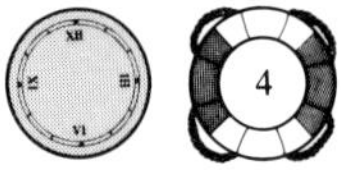

4 potatoes, chopped
2 onions, sliced
1–3 fish fillets, cut into pieces
2 small cans of evaporated milk
$\frac{1}{2}$ stick (2 oz) of butter or margarine
salt and pepper

Boil the potatoes and onions until thoroughly cooked, then add the fish. When it is soft, add the milk, butter, salt and pepper. Let the soup stand for at least an hour before serving.

Labskaus

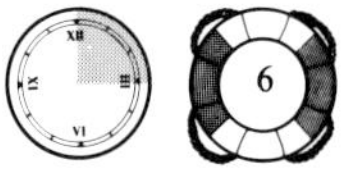

2 pounds of mashed potatoes
4 small herrings
1 pound of corned beef, sliced in strips
1 bottle of pickled beetroot
2 dill pickles, sliced
2 onions, sliced
2 tablespoons cooking oil
salt and pepper

Brown the onions in cooking oil, then add the corned beef, pickles and mashed potatoes. Heat, mix and serve with herrings and pickled beet on top.

Scrapple

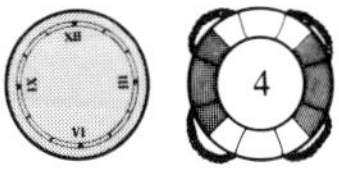

$\frac{1}{2}$–$\frac{3}{4}$ pound salami
1 cup cornmeal
2–3 garlic cloves, diced
1 quart salted water

Boil the water – which can be half sea water, half fresh – and mix in all ingredients. Then place in a double boiler and cook for at least an hour. Cool, slice and fry in an open pan until brown.

Anchovies in a Bucket

Take 3–4 kilos of fresh anchovies and place them in layers in a bucket, sprinkling a handful of rock salt on each layer. Cover the fish with a circular piece of wood which fits inside the bucket. Put a heavy stone on it, and leave it for about ten days.

Then pour off the juice, take out the fish, clean them, cut off the heads and tails and replace them in the bucket with a little new salt. Add the juice, cover again with the wood and stone and store. After about four weeks the taste is fantastic.

Curry

Almost anything can be curried – meat, fish, vegetables, even eggs. It is the Cook's all-purpose seasoning. However, curry is not one spice, but a blend. Its flavour can vary from mild and sweet to hot and tangy, depending on how it is mixed.

A basic formula is:

1 tablespoon coriander
1 tablespoon cumin
1 tablespoon saffron
½ tablespoon nutmeg
1 teaspoon cayenne
1 teaspoon cardamom

Cinnamon, cloves, ginger, mustard seed and turmeric can also be added. To find just the right blend for your taste, we recommend a little experimentation.

Chapter 2

A Boat Full of Landlubbers

'*one day the head teachers of Papauta College, Miss Schultze and Miss Moore, came on board with their ninety-seven young women students. They were all dressed in white, and each wore a red rose, and of course came in boats or canoes in the cold-climate style. A merrier bevy of girls it would be difficult to find. As soon as they got on deck, by request of one of the teachers, they sang* The Watch on the Rhine, *which I had never heard before. "And now," said they all, "let's up anchor and away."*'

Joshua Slocum, Sailing Alone Around the World

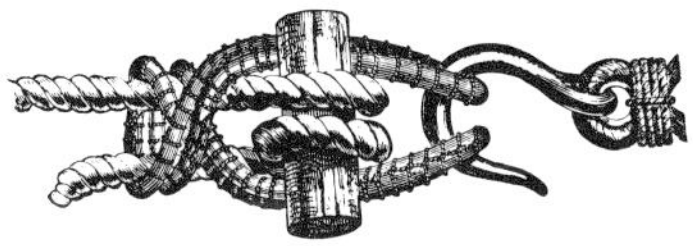

Next Saturday the worst is scheduled to occur. A troop of Sea Scouts, your wife and her Garden Club, an old grade school-teacher and her extended family, your daughter's giggling class-mates, two former girl-friends and your psychoanalyst have all invited themselves for a day's cruise.

Unfortunately, the engine had just been repaired, and the weather, which has been terrible for the last two months, will probably clear by the weekend. There are no excuses on the horizon.

The mob will take over the boat. That's certain. They'll scar the varnish work, spill suntan oil on the deck and foul every line they touch. The only place for you to hide is in the galley.

Sandwiches

Roquefort sandwich	*rye bread* *Roquefort cheese* *chopped celery* *olives* *chives*
Bambinowich	*creamed cheese* *pineapple ring*
Reubin	*sauerkraut* *Swiss cheese* *corned beef* *Thousand Island dressing*

Sandwich Spreads

Tarragona Tuna

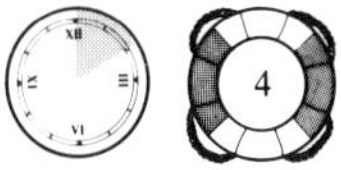

1 small can tuna fish
1 onion, chopped
½ green pepper, chopped
2 hard-boiled eggs, chopped
6 green olives, diced

Salmon Crumble

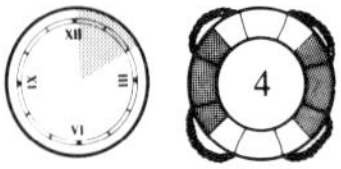

1 small can of salmon
1 small jar of capers, diced
mayonnaise
handful of breadcrumbs

Sardinian Sardine

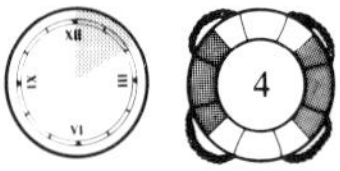

2 cans of sardines in tomato sauce
3 hard-boiled eggs, chopped
1 tablespoon mayonnaise
dash of lemon juice

Tunafish Loaf

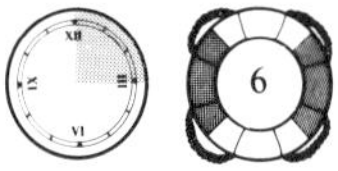

2 pounds potatoes, mashed
2 small cans of tuna
¾ cup (6 tablespoons) of mayonnaise
2 green peppers, diced
4 hard-boiled eggs
6–8 olives

Break the tuna into small pieces and mix with the potatoes and green pepper. Stir in the mayonnaise. Press the mixture into a greased bread tin, then turn out on to a serving dish. Spread a little mayonnaise on the top, and garnish with olives and egg slices.

Alberto's Noodle Salad

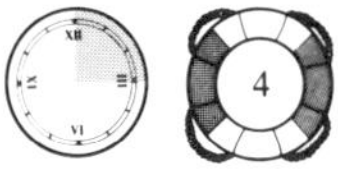

1 pound cooked noodles or macaroni
1 pound salami, chopped
2 apples, sliced
3 dill pickles, diced
1 green pepper, chopped
juice of one lemon
handful of green olives
1 teaspoon soya sauce
dash of olive oil
salt
pepper

Double Cabbage Salad

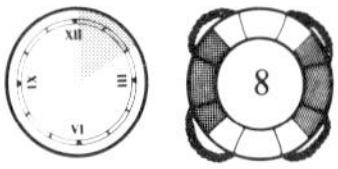

1 head white cabbage
1 head red cabbage
2 green peppers, sliced
2 apples, sliced
2 oranges in sections
juice of ½ lemon
3 tablespoons mayonnaise
3 tablespoons condensed milk
palmful of chopped nuts

Slice the cabbage, and mix all ingredients together.

Hot Potato Salad

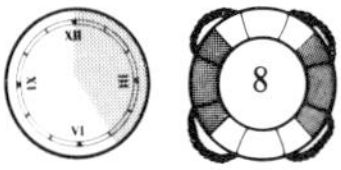

3 pounds potatoes
½ pound bacon, chopped
2 onions, chopped
2 tablespoons wine vinegar
¼ cup water
palmful of chopped parsley
salt
pepper

Boil and peel the potatoes. Fry the bacon, remove from the pan and brown onions in bacon fat. Add vinegar, water, salt and pepper, and let cook for one minute. Pour sauce over potatoes, sprinkle on pieces of bacon and parsley and serve immediately.

Basic Spaghetti

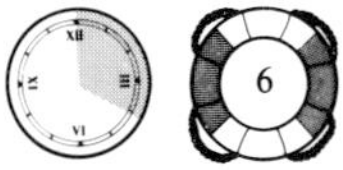

1 pound of spaghetti or noodles
4 tablespoons butter or margarine
2 onions, chopped
1½ cups sour cream
salt and pepper

Cook and drain the spaghetti, then place it in a warm bowl. Melt the butter in a frying pan and sauté the onions. Add sour cream. When hot, season to taste, then mix with the spaghetti.

2–4 tablespoons of a strong cheese, such as blue or Roquefort, can be used instead of sour cream.

Risotto

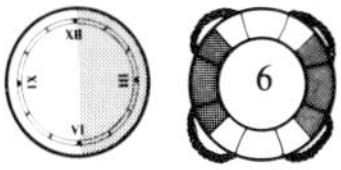

1 pound rice
1 onion, chopped
1 green pepper, chopped
2 small cans chicken soup
4 tablespoons butter or margarine
¼ cup (3 tablespoons) grated cheese, preferably Parmesan

Melt butter in a saucepan, add onion and pepper and sauté. Stir in the rice and cook until shiny. Then pour in chicken soup – it may be necessary to thin it with water – bring to the boil, cover and let cook for 15–20 minutes. Add the cheese just before serving.

Ham, Eggs and Macaroni

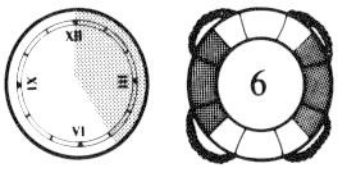

6 eggs
½ pound ham, diced
1 pound macaroni
¼ cup (3 tablespoons) Parmesan or other grated cheese

Cook the macaroni, strain it and put it in a warm bowl. Then beat the eggs and fry them with the ham as if an omelette. Just as the eggs begin to solidify pour them over the macaroni. Sprinkle on the cheese, stir a few times and serve.

Sun-deck Tea

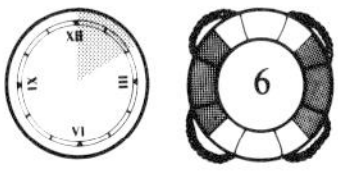

8 teaspoons black tea
3 cups water
1 small can of pineapple, rings or chunks
½ cup sugar
juice of 3 lemons

Boil the tea and let it cool. Add lemon juice, sugar and the syrup from the pineapple, then the chopped pineapple pieces. Serve cold.

Rice

When stored in a cool, dry, well-ventilated place rice will keep for years. Before buying by the sackful, however, cook a sample batch, for rice can vary enormously in taste and quality.

Rice should be washed before it is cooked in order to remove the starch which can make it sticky. If you like rice with a bleached appearance, add a few drops of lemon juice during cooking.

As a general rule, cooked rice swells to three times its original size. The common methods of preparation are:

1 Bring a pot of salted water to a boil; add a few tablespoons of oil and the washed rice, then let it cook for 15–20 minutes. Drain off the water, place the rice in a casserole and put it in a hot oven for a few minutes.

2 Bring a pot of salted water to a boil; add the washed rice, then let it cook until the rice is tender – about 25–30 minutes.

3 Heat margarine or oil in a pot; add the washed rice and stir until it is glazed and slightly brown. Pour in boiling water or bouillon and simmer for about 30 minutes. If the liquid steams away, add more.

An easy way to re-heat left-over rice without its becoming soggy is: put it in a strainer and place it over a pot of boiling water.

Reserve Store

Every yacht should have a box of food set aside for an emergency, be it an unexpected storm, a broken engine or just an extra day in a secluded anchorage.

A basic reserve store ought to include:

Powdered milk
Tinned or well-packaged dried bread
One-pot meals in tins
Tinned margarine
Honey
Marmalade
Sugar
Biscuits
Oatflakes
Powdered potatoes
Corned beef
Beer
Fruit juice
Olives

Yoghurt

Yoghurt is a natural food, easy to digest, highly nutritious and very simple to make. But you will need a small container of yoghurt to start with.

Heat two cups of milk (fresh or powdered) to boiling point, then add three tablespoons of unflavoured gelatin which has been dissolved in $\frac{1}{4}$ cup of warm water. Mix in two cups of cool milk and about three tablespoons of plain yoghurt. (The remainder of the previous batch of yoghurt can be used.) Pour into a jar, cover tightly, wrap in a blanket or towels and let sit for eight to ten hours.

For a creamy yoghurt double the ratio of milk powder to water.

When stored in a cool bilge, yoghurt will keep for at least three to four days.

Chapter 3

The Day's Catch

'You did not kill the fish only to keep alive and to sell for food, he thought. You killed him for pride and because you are a fisherman. You loved him when he was alive and you loved him after. If you love him, it is not a sin to kill him. Or is it more?'

Ernest Hemingway, The Old Man and the Sea

'What you think is meat, Professor, is nothing but sea-turtle steak. Here also are some dolphin livers which you should think were stewed pork. I have an excellent cook, whose specialty is preparing sea food. Take a taste of all these dishes. Here are sea cucumbers we put up in jars and which a Malayan would declare unrivalled in the whole world, here is cream made from whale's milk, and sugar extracted from rock weed in the North Sea, and lastly permit me to offer you anemone jam, which is as good as that made from the most delicious fruit.

I tasted all these things more out of curiosity than as a connoisseur, while Captain Nemo regaled me with his unlikely stories.'

Jules Verne, 20,000 Leagues Under the Sea

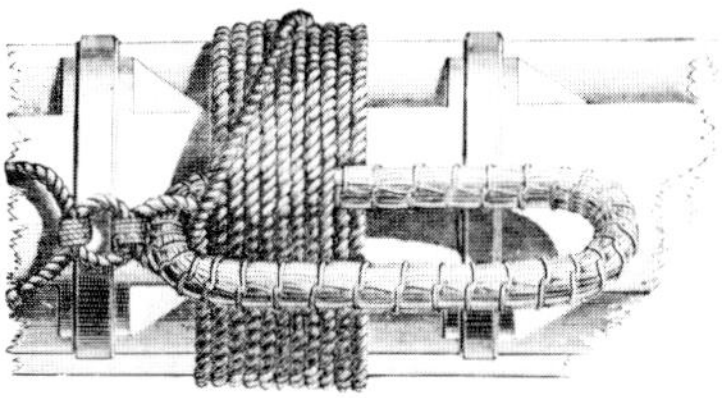

Even with the most expensive tackle, the best advice, the newest fish finder and perfect weather, when the hook drops into the water, luck takes over. But this need not be discouraging. Like fate and destiny, luck can be tempted. But that calls for the Cook.

Sometimes a bit of his greasy towel tied to the leader is enough, or a mixture of dishwater, rum and brown sugar pumped through the sink's sea-cock. Greek cooks often recite an ode to Neptune, and on Portuguese ships the cook smears the hook with garlic. In New Guinea he places a drawing of the fish in a frying pan before the line goes over the side.

In any case, one thing is clear. Behind every good fisherman is a good Cook.

Fish Butters

Herb butter

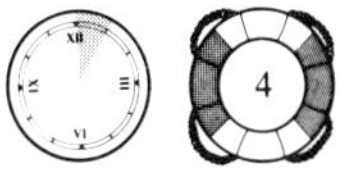

1 onion, minced
2 garlic cloves, crushed
½ teaspoon lemon juice
1 stick (¼ pound) butter or margarine
palmful of chopped chives
palmful of chopped parsley
salt and pepper

Cream the butter with a fork and slowly add the rest of the ingredients. Mould into pats and serve alongside each portion.

Mustard butter

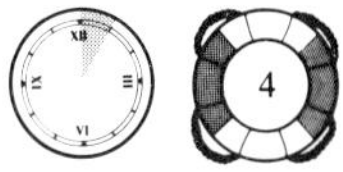

1 stick (¼ pound) of butter or margarine
1 teaspoon prepared mustard
dash of mustard powder
dash of pepper

Garlic butter

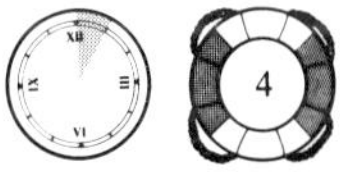

1 stick (¼ pound) butter or margarine
2 garlic cloves, crushed
salt and pepper

Curry butter

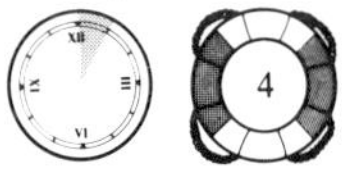

1 stick (¼ pound) butter or margarine
1–3 pinches of curry powder

Tomato butter

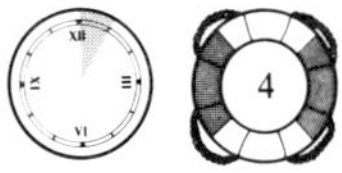

1 stick (¼ pound) butter or margarine
3 teaspoons tomato paste
pinch of sugar
salt and pepper

Tarragon butter

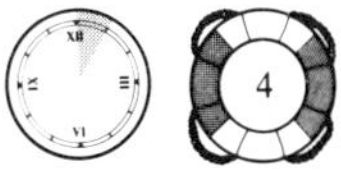

1 stick (¼ pound) butter or margarine
palmful of chopped chives
1 teaspoon tarragon

Cocktail Sauce

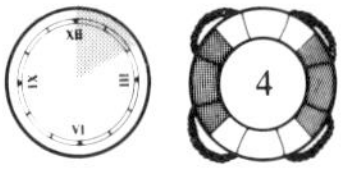

½ cup (catsup) ketchup
1 tablespoon horseradish
pinch of mustard
1 tablespoon Worcestershire sauce
½ teaspoon chilli powder
salt and pepper

Mix all ingredients, being careful not to add too much chilli powder.

Mayonnaise

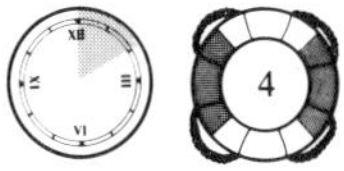

2 egg yolks
½ teaspoon dry mustard
¾ cup olive oil
juice of one lemon
pinch of salt

Place egg yolks, salt and mustard in a bowl and beat well, slowly adding the olive oil. When the mixture has thickened, add lemon juice.

For Green Mayonnaise: add finely chopped parsley, chives, tarragon or watercress.

Béchamel Sauce

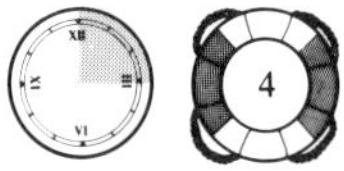

1½ cups milk
1 onion, chopped
2 tablespoons flour
2 tablespoons butter or margarine
dash of salt

Melt the butter in a frying pan, add onion and cook until soft. Then add flour, salt and milk. Cook until the mixture thickens.

Hawaiian Fish Sauce

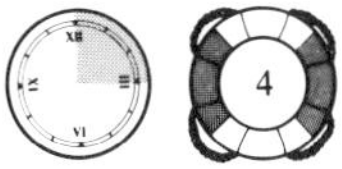

1 small can of pineapple, crushed or chunks
2 tablespoons lemon juice
pinch of curry powder

Mix well and pour over the fish.

Tartare Sauce

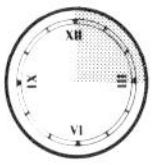
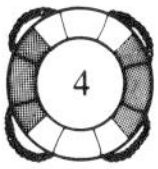

1 cup mayonnaise
1 teaspoon lemon juice
1 small onion, chopped
1 palmful chopped parsley
1 palmful diced dill pickle

Start with the mayonnaise, then add the other ingredients, lemon juice, onion, pickle and lastly, the parsley. Let stand for several hours before serving.

Thousand Island Dressing

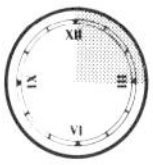
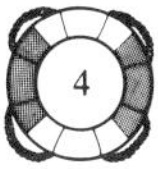

1 cup mayonnaise
1 small onion, chopped
1 hard-boiled egg, chopped
1 palmful chopped parsley
3–4 tablespoons (catsup) ketchup
1 teaspoon dry mustard
pinch of chilli powder

Mix all ingredients, adding the chilli powder last. Let stand for several hours before serving.

Curry Sauce

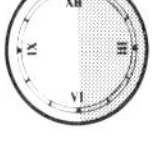
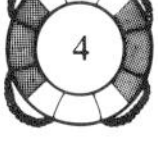

1 tablespoon curry powder
½ cup white wine
1 onion, sliced
¼ stick butter or margarine
1 tomato, peeled, sliced
½ apple, cored, sliced
½ cup milk
¼ cup grated coconut

Cook the onions in butter until soft, then add apple, tomatoes, curry powder and wine. Simmer for 10 minutes, then add the coconut. Cook over a low flame for 10 minutes more. For a perfectly smooth sauce, pour through a strainer. Add powdered milk or flour to thicken, if necessary.

Sauce Aïoli

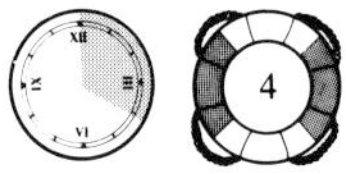

At least 12 large garlic cloves
4 egg yolks
1 cup olive oil
juice of one lemon
salt

Crush the garlic, preferably in a mortar, then slowly add the egg yolks. Pour in the olive oil gradually until the sauce becomes thick as mayonnaise. Lastly, add the salt and lemon juice.

Sweet and Sour Sauce

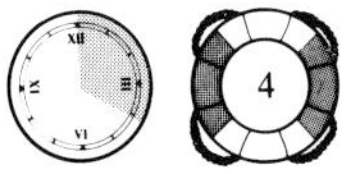

1 large can pineapple chunks
1 cup vinegar
½ cup brown sugar
1½ cups water
¼ cup cornflour (cornstarch)

Mix sugar, vinegar and water and thicken with cornflour (cornstarch) and the juice from pineapple. Cook, stirring constantly, for 10–15 minutes, or until the sauce has thickened. Add the pineapple chunks and pour over the fish.

Hollandaise Sauce

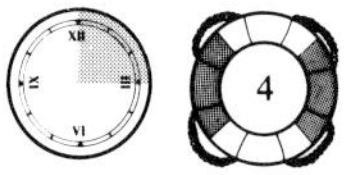

4 egg yolks
1 stick (¼ pound) butter or margarine
3 tablespoons lemon juice
dash of pepper

Cook the ingredients over a low flame, stirring constantly. The sauce should reach a proper consistency in 2–3 minutes. If too thick, thin with milk.

Basic Batter

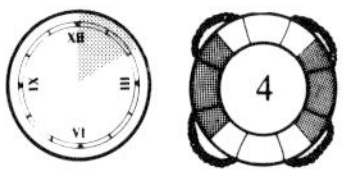

¼ pound flour
3 tablespoons olive oil
white of one egg
pinch of salt
½ cup water

Mix olive oil, flour, water and salt into a thick cream, then let stand for several hours. Stir in the beaten egg white just before using.

Fillet of Fish – any kind – à la Crème

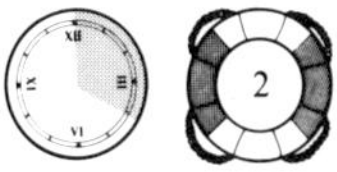

1 piece fish fillet
1 onion, sliced
1 glass of white wine
1 glass of water
½–¾ cup of cream
palmful of parsley or chives
salt and pepper

Poach the fillet in a frying pan in a mixture of wine and water. Sprinkle with onions. When fish is cooked, probably about 10 minutes, remove from pan. Boil liquid in pan until it equals the amount of cream. Then add cream, bring to the boil again and serve with a sprinkling of parsley.

Camargue Fish Stew

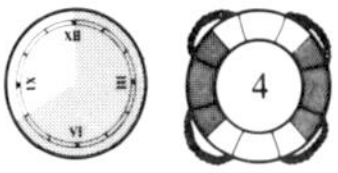

2 pounds fish, any kind, chopped in small pieces
2 onions, chopped
4 tomatoes, sliced
2 garlic cloves, crushed
4 carrots, chopped
2 celery stalks, chopped
4 tablespoons olive oil
1 glass white wine
4 slices white bread
2 potatoes, chopped
2 bouillon cubes
1 tablespoon butter
handful of parsley

Fry the onions, tomatoes, garlic and celery in the oil until they begin to soften. Add the fish, wine, bouillon and potatoes, and let the mixture steam slowly. In another pan, fry the bread in butter, then lay the slices on top of the stew, sprinkle with parsley and serve.

Simple Bouillabaisse

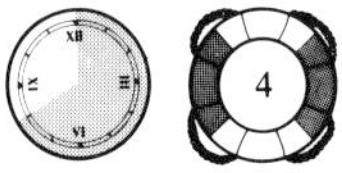

2 cups olive oil
5 onions, quartered
5 garlic cloves
2 green peppers, sliced
1 stalk of celery, sliced
1 carrot, sliced
3 tomatoes, quartered
10 green olives, stoned (pitted)
2 pounds fish, at least two kinds, chopped in small pieces
1 cup white wine
pinch of saffron
2–3 bay leaves
salt and pepper

Fry the onions and garlic in olive oil. Add the chopped vegetables – tomatoes, olives, carrots, celery and green peppers – fish and shellfish, and let simmer, while stirring gently so that cooking is even. Add salt, pepper and bay leaves. Also wine and water until the mixture is covered. Simmer for five minutes more, add saffron and serve in bowls.

Fishing Tips

1 Always experiment. Change lures, colours, fishing depth, speed, bait and length of line. Beyond a strong hook, some stainless steel leader, and strong line there are no absolutes.

2 Rubber bands or strips of inner tubes make an excellent shock absorber, and can indicate when a fish is on the line.

3 In our experience, yellow, white or silver lures are best early in the morning or at sunset; brightly coloured ones during the day.

4 Trail as many lines as possible. We found two to be about all we could handle, however. Whenever possible, we ran one line off the end of the boom or an outrigged bamboo pole so as not to tangle the log.

5 Take the lines in at night unless you're on deck to watch them. A dead fish with an open mouth on the hook is like a sea anchor, and you could lose all your tackle.

6 The most critical moment is usually getting your fish on board. Never pull it up by the line; always use a gaff or a net.

Fishing Lures

Lures are easily lost and these days quite expensive to replace. It's much cheaper to make your own and aside from the hook, more than likely all the material you need is already on board.

A simple and amazingly effective lure can be made by unravelling about 20 centimetres of thick rope and lashing it to a wire leader. Since apparently fish are attracted to colour, a few strips of brightly coloured plastic should be tied on each side.

If you don't want to waste some of your best line, a few pieces of old towel or a shopping bag's worth of plastic, cut into thin strips, will often work just as well.

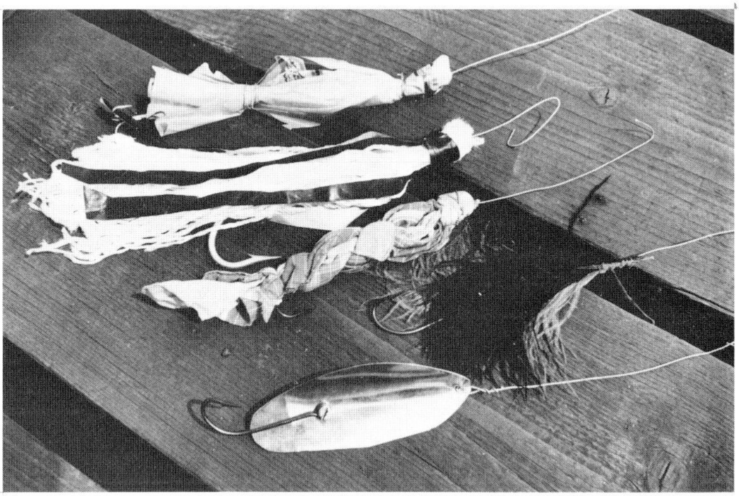

And should you be having flying fish for breakfast, saving one to use as a lure may be more profitable than putting it in your stomach. But be sure to pass the leader through the fish's body and then sew the mouth closed.

Dipped Half Blood-knot (The Fisherman's Bowline)

A fishing line is as strong as its weakest knot. For attaching weights, swivels and hooks to line we used this knot which only reduces the strength of the line by about 3%. An overhand knot, by contrast, reduces the strength of the line by 40% to 60%.

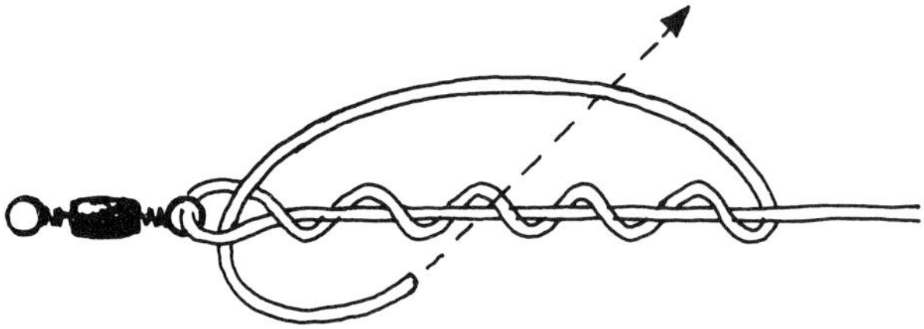

Fresh Fish

Seafood of all kinds is perhaps the most perishable food in the world. Once taken from the water, it begins to deteriorate almost immediately. It should be cleaned at once, all blood drained off, and kept as cool as possible. A fish that is fresh will have clear and bulging eyes, firm flesh, pink or reddish gills, shiny scales, and no strong odour. As soon as a fish begins to decay, the oils oxidize causing a strong, rancid smell and a bitter taste. Since harmful bacteria and enzymes multiply rapidly, it is always best to throw a questionable fish over the side.

Dried Fish

When your luck outruns your appetite and you've too much fish on board, one solution is to dry it. For small fish, those of two kilos or less, chop off the heads and tails, clean them and break the backbones so that the fish is flat. Lay them in the sun, sprinkle on some salt and turn occasionally until the meat begins to dry. Then string them on a line, and hang them between the shrouds. When they become hard, store below, either in an open-weave basket or between the deck beams.

To use: soak the pieces in fresh water for a day, changing the water at least twice.

For larger fish, debone as much as possible, cut into strips or fillets, and follow the same process.

Chapter 4

A Weekend Cruise

'Do you mean to tell me, Mr. Hornblower,' said the Chief Commissary, 'That you allowed your men to eat fresh beef? A bullock a day for your eighteen men? There must have been plenty of ship's provisions on board. That was wanton extravagance, Mr. Hornblower, I'm surprised at you.'

C. S. Forester, Mr. Midshipman Hornblower

'Well, Joe, it was a great voyage. And what meals! I haven't enjoyed food like that in years.'

'That's what sailing is all about, Ed. Good food and plenty of it.'

'I've got to admit your soufflé was superb. And the ratatouille! Fantastic! You know, Joe, for me the high point of the weekend was not when we blew out the mainsail or the mast went overboard, but when you put that platter of curried tuna on the table. That's a moment I'll never forget.'

'Oh, it was nothing, Ed. Just a few tins and a pinch of imagination.'

'You're not much of a captain, but one hell of a good cook.'

'Why don't you come along next weekend? I'm going to prepare a paella.'

'Put me on the crew list. I never knew sailing could be so exciting.'

Beer Soup One

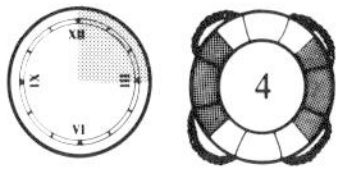

4 cups light (beer) ale
2 tablespoons sugar
4 egg yolks
4 tablespoons sour cream
½ teaspoon cinnamon
salt and pepper

Heat the beer and sugar in a large casserole until the sugar is dissolved. Let the mixture boil, then remove from the stove. Put the egg yolks in a bowl, beat them and slowly add the sour cream. Then add four tablespoons of hot beer, and mix thoroughly. Pour into the casserole, season with cinnamon, salt and pepper, then cook on a low flame for a few minutes. Serve hot.

Dutch Potato Salad

2 pounds potatoes, cooked and peeled
1 onion, chopped
handful of chopped celery
¼ cup mayonnaise
2 tablespoons oil
2 tablespoons vinegar
1 teaspoon lemon juice
salt and pepper

Cut the potatoes into chunks and place in a bowl with celery and onion. For the sauce, combine mayonnaise, lemon juice, oil, vinegar and salt and pepper. Mix well, and pour over the potatoes.

Drunken Spaghetti

1 pound spaghetti
3 fingers cognac
3 garlic cloves, crushed
½ stick (2 oz) butter or margarine
½ teaspoon white pepper

Put garlic and cognac in a glass and let stand for about half an hour. Then cook spaghetti, dry it and place it in a warm bowl. Mix in butter and pepper. Remove garlic from the cognac, pour it over the spaghetti, mix and serve immediately.

Curried Tuna Fish

1 small can tuna fish, or several cooked, chopped fillets
1 small can mushroom soup
1 teaspoon curry powder
1 medium can green peas

Mix fish and soup in a casserole, add curry and drained peas. Bake for about 15–20 minutes, and serve over rice or noodles.

Fried Cheese

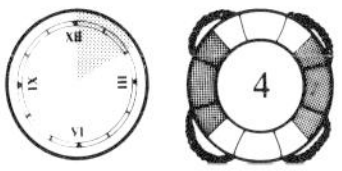

10–12 slices white cheese, cut into thin strips
3 tablespoons flour
1 egg
3 tablespoons breadcrumbs
2 tablespoons cooking oil

Dust cheese strips with flour, dip into the beaten egg, coat with breadcrumbs and fry in hot oil, turning only once.

Eggs Bombay

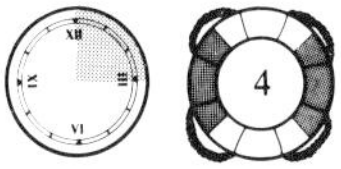

8 hard-boiled eggs, cut in quarters
1 onion, chopped
1 cup milk
2 tablespoons flour
2 tablespoons butter or margarine
2–4 tablespoons curry powder
pinch of salt

Cook the onion in butter, then add the flour and the milk. Stir constantly until the sauce is thick and creamy. Add the curry powder and salt, then the eggs. Mix gently, and serve over toast or muffins.

Chicken-Liver Snack

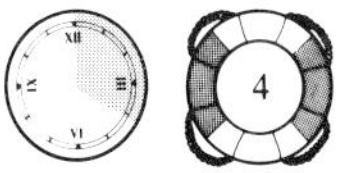

1 pound chopped chicken livers
1 onion, chopped
1 green pepper, chopped
¼ stick (1 oz) butter or margarine
5 rashers (slices) bacon
2 teaspoons paprika
½ teaspoon salt

Cook the bacon in a frying pan, then add butter, onions and green peppers. Simmer for about 10 minutes. When onions are soft and brown, add the chicken livers, cover and cook for about 5 minutes. Add the paprika and salt and serve.

Ratatouille

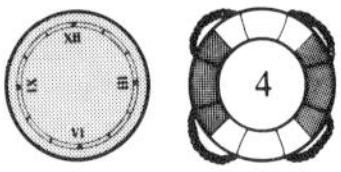

2 onions, sliced
1 green pepper, sliced
2 tomatoes, sliced
2 cloves of garlic, minced
1 bunch of parsley
3–4 tablespoons olive oil
pinch of rosemary
1 cup white wine
1 aubergine (egg plant), sliced
salt and pepper

Heat the oil in a casserole, add all the vegetables, rosemary and garlic. Mix well, then pour in wine. Simmer slowly until the vegetables begin to soften. If necessary add a bit more wine. Be careful not to overcook.

Pancakes

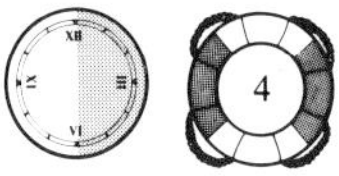

3 eggs
1 cup milk
1 teaspoon salt
1¼ cups flour
2 tablespoons melted butter, margarine or oil

Mix flour and salt. Add eggs, melted butter and beat in the milk. If possible, let the batter stand for several hours before using.

Variations:

1. Add diced apples, cherries or pineapples to the batter.
2. After turning the pancakes coat with grated cheese.
3. Add leftover chopped meat, bacon or sausage.

Welsh Rarebit (Rabbit)

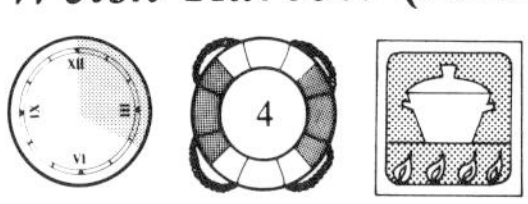

4 slices toast
½ pound grated cheese
1 tablespoon flour
1 egg yolk
2 tablespoons beer

1 tablespoon butter
1 teaspoon Worcestershire sauce
pinch of cayenne pepper
1 teaspoon mustard

Mix cheese, flour, butter, Worcestershire sauce, mustard and pepper in a large casserole, heat, but do not boil. Stir constantly. When cheese has melted, add egg yolk. Put toast in a greased baking tin, and pour the sauce over it. Bake in a moderate oven until golden brown.

Apple Meatloaf

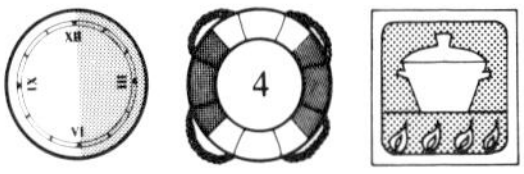

1 pound minced (hamburger) meat
1 cup cooked rice
1 beaten egg
1 dash Worcestershire sauce
1 small can apple rings or sauce
1 tablespoon lemon juice
2 tablespoons cornflour (cornstarch)
salt and pepper

Mix minced (hamburger) beef, rice, egg, Worcestershire sauce, salt and pepper. Add a little water, if necessary. Shape into patties and place in a greased baking tin. Put apple rings, or drained sauce, on top of the patties and bake in a moderate oven for about half an hour. Mix the apple syrup, cornflour (cornstarch) and lemon juice in a frying pan, adding 2–3 tablespoons water until the mixture thickens. Pour over the meat just before serving.

McAdam's Corn Biscuits

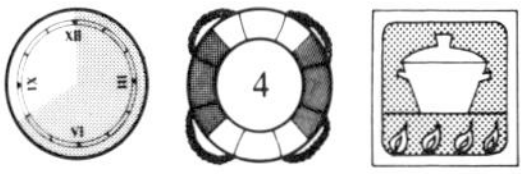

½ cup cornmeal
½ cup boiling water
2 beaten egg whites
pinch of salt

Mix water, cornmeal and salt into a mush. Fold in egg whites, and drop, like cookies, on to a greased baking pan or sheet. Bake in a moderate oven for about half an hour.

Highlands Shortbread

2 cups flour
1 cup butter
$\frac{1}{2}$ cup sugar
handful chopped nuts

Using your hands, work sugar and butter together. Slowly add flour. Press the dough into a greased baking pan until it is about $\frac{1}{4}$ inch thick. With a fork, prick a decorative design, sprinkle on nuts and bake in a moderate oven for about 20 minutes.

A Few Notes on Eggs

Eggs are an excellent meat substitute. Five eggs contain as much protein as half a pound of beef.

To determine whether an egg is fresh, drop it into a litre of water mixed with a $\frac{1}{4}$ pound of salt. If the egg sinks, it is fresh; if it floats midway to the top, it is at least several days old; if it rises to the surface, it is too old to use.

Since egg shells are porous they will absorb smells. Therefore, do not store them near anything which has a strong odour.

Deep-Fat Frying

Deep-fat frying commonly results in greasy varnish work, glazed portholes and dirty ceilings. A practical way to avoid this is to cover the frying pan with an old newspaper, which will soak up the excess grease. Be careful to keep the edges of the paper well out of reach of the flame.

Bread

When the crew is tired of hard tack and mouldy ship's biscuits, it's time for the Cook to turn his galley into a bakery. Although the process is a bit time consuming, bread-making is actually quite simple and straightforward. The basic ingredients are flour, liquid (milk/water), salt, sugar, dried yeast and oil or shortening. By varying the proportions, more sugar and shortening, rolls, cakes and pastry become possible. Just the freshly baked smell wafting out of the galley makes all the effort worthwhile.

Chapter 5

Kids as Crew

'Captain Nemo brought the Nautilus *alongside the cadaver. Two of his men got off on the the whale and, to my great surprise, started milking her. By the time they were through, they had enough to fill two or three casks.*

The captain offered me a glass of this still warm milk. I could not refrain from showing my distaste for this sort of drink. But he assured me that it was not only excellent, but indistinguishable from cow's milk.

I tasted it and was forced to agree with him. It therefore provided us with a useful reserve stock, for this milk – in the form of salted butter or cheese – brought a pleasant change in our usual diet.'

Jules Verne, 20,000 Leagues Under the Sea

Dear Stephen,

I'am having a wonderful time this
summer on my brother's boat. I've seen
whales, sharks and dolphins.
I'm also learning how to sail.
Yesterday, I caught my first tuna. It was
almost as big as I am.
You wouldn't believe how well we eat –
so many things I've never tasted before–
apple sandwiches, flying fish pizza,
chocolate soup, and coconut bread.
I don't even miss ice cream.
I hope you're having a good time on
the farm

Love
Jesse

P.S. I may be a little late for the beginning
of school.

Chocolate Soup

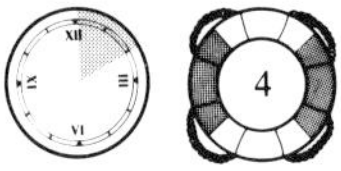

¼ pound chocolate, grated
3 cups milk
1 tablespoon flour
3 tablespoons sugar
pinch of salt

Using a little milk, mix flour and chocolate. Boil the rest of the milk with sugar and salt, then stir in the chocolate – flour mixture and let it boil for 2–4 minutes. Serve hot.

Chocolate Oatmeal

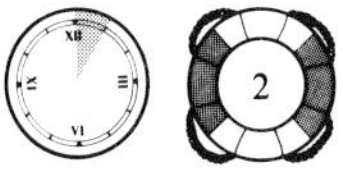

6 tablespoons oatmeal
2 teaspoons cocoa
4 teaspoons brown sugar
1 cup milk

Mix the dry ingredients together, then pour in the milk and heat until oatmeal is soft.

Honey and Banana Toast

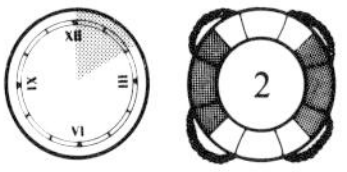

4 bananas
½ teaspoon lemon juice
2 tablespoons honey
4 slices buttered toast
1 tablespoon crushed nuts

Using a fork, mash bananas in a bowl. Add lemon juice and honey. Spread mixture over the toast, then place in a hot oven for about 3 minutes. Sprinkle on nuts and serve hot.

Apple Sandwiches

several apples, peeled and cored
ham or cheese, sliced

Cut the apples into rounds of about a finger's thickness. Place cheese or ham between two rounds and serve as a sandwich.

Popeye's Sugar Cookies

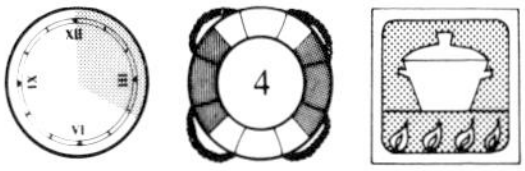

3 cups flour
1 cup sugar
3 teaspoons baking powder
1 teaspoon vanilla essence (extract)
2 eggs
pinch of salt
½ cup shortening

Combine the shortening and sugar, then add eggs, baking powder, flour and salt. Mix well, and pour in vanilla. Roll out on a floured board, cut into shapes, sprinkle with sugar and bake on a greased sheet in a hot oven for about 10 minutes.

Popcorn Buoys

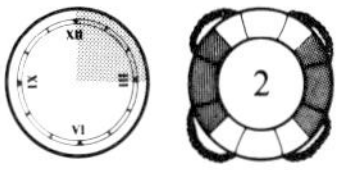

½ cup popcorn
¼ cup cooking oil
½ cup corn syrup
½ cup sugar
pinch of salt

Heat oil and pop popcorn. In a bowl, mix the corn syrup, sugar and salt, then add it to the popcorn. Stir well until all the popcorn is covered, then remove from stove. Coat your hands with cooking oil, and mould the popcorn into balls.

Banana Paté

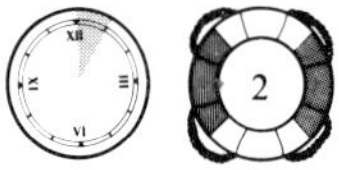

2 large bananas
2 tablespoons condensed milk
1 teaspoon honey
1 teaspoon lemon juice
3 tablespoons oatmeal

Mash the bananas, then combine with milk. Mix in the rest of the ingredients and serve.

Jam Omelette

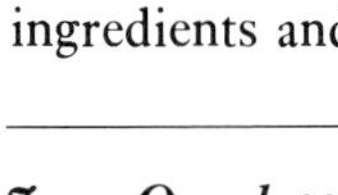

4 eggs
2 tablespoons butter
4 tablespoons jam – any kind
¼ cup milk
salt and pepper

Mix eggs and milk together in a bowl. Season, then pour into a hot, buttered frying pan. When the eggs are half cooked, spread the jam in a strip, fold in the sides, turn and cook until eggs are firm.

Nora's Macaroons

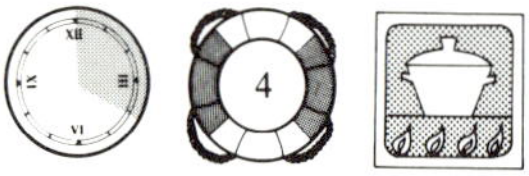

1 pound almond paste
8 egg whites
2 tablespoons flour
1¼ pounds sugar

Work the paste and sugar together – it's best to use your hands. Add the unbeaten egg whites, one at a time. Mix well. Then stir in the flour. Drop on to a greased baking sheet, and bake in a moderate oven for about 15–20 minutes.

Sail Cookies

1 cup butter
2 cups flour
½ cup brown sugar

Work butter and sugar together, and gradually add the flour. When dough is mixed and stiff, roll on a floured board and cut into triangular shapes. Bake on a greased sheet for 15 minutes in a moderate oven.

Cracker Jacks

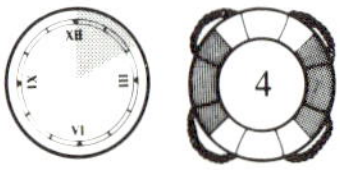

2 quarts popcorn, popped
1 cup molasses
½ cup sugar
2 cups peanuts, shelled

Heat popcorn and peanuts in a pan. In another, mix molasses and sugar until the syrup becomes threadlike when dropped in water. Pour syrup over popcorn and peanuts, mix well, then break into chunks. Let cool and serve.

Candy Apples

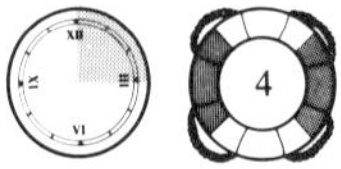

4 medium-sized apples
4 iced-lolly (popsicle) sticks
1 cup sugar
½ cup corn syrup
¼ cup water
handful of cinnamon candies
5 drops red food colouring

Mix sugar, corn syrup and water in a saucepan, stirring constantly until the mixture boils and sugar is dissolved. Let boil for approximately one minute. Add cinnamon candies. Let cook another half minute, then remove from heat. Add food colouring. Skewer the apples, swirl them in the mixture, then let them dry on a greased baking sheet or waxed paper.

Variations:

1 Add one drop of cinnamon oil for a tangier flavour.

2 Instead of water, cinnamon candies and food colouring, use one small can of condensed milk, and a teaspoon of vanilla extract to make caramel apples. Heat at least five minutes after boiling before dipping apples.

Salt-water Taffy

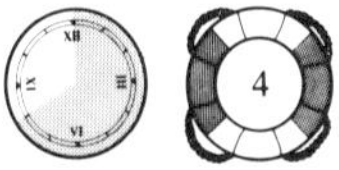

1 tablespoon cornflour (cornstarch)
1 cup corn syrup
2 tablespoons butter
¾ cup water
pinch of salt
2 cups sugar

Heat sugar, cornflour (cornstarch), corn syrup, butter and water and stir until mixture comes to the boil. Let boil, without stirring for approximately one minute. Add salt and pour on to a buttered platter. When cooled – PULL! (Taffy is pulled usually by two persons, one acting as a hook, the other stretching the taffy again and again until it takes on a whitish colour.) Then divide into portions, add flavouring and colouring, if desired, serve or wrap in waxed paper.

A Cocktail for Dwarfs

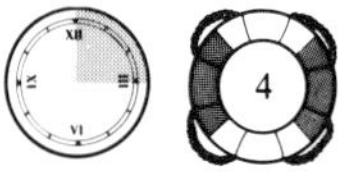

1 large can pineapple juice
1 bottle ginger ale
8 cloves
1 teaspoon cinnamon
1 cup water
1 cup orange juice
$\frac{2}{3}$ cup sugar

Heat the sugar, water, cinnamon and cloves, and simmer for 10 minutes. Cool and strain out the spices. Then add the pineapple juice, orange juice and lastly the ginger ale. Serve cold.

Dry Ice

When packed with water ice, dry ice will turn a styroform ice chest into a deep freeze which will retain its cooling power for a week. A rough formula is: a slab of dry ice equal to one-tenth the water ice. But handle it carefully as it is extremely cold (-109°F.). Since dry ice is a chemical compound which releases carbon dioxide, the ice-chest lid should not be tightly clamped down. Also anyone suffering from sea-sickness should be kept far away as the smell often intensifies the malady.

Caring for Matches

For some inexplicable reason, it always seems to require at least ten matches to light a stove on board a yacht. Matches are one item that should definitely be purchased by the case. It's wise to break them into packs of 5 or 10, seal them in plastic and store them in different places on the boat. But don't forget to make a list of where you've stored them, and buy a throwaway lighter just in case.

Bean Sprouts

Nearly any kind of bean can be sprouted, but perhaps the most tasty are alfalfa, soya and mung. Especially on a long voyage, they provide a source of vitamins and fresh food.
There are several methods of preparation:

1 Wrap a handful of beans in a cheesecloth and place it in a bowl. Moisten it at least three times a day. After three days your harvest is ready.

2 Spread a handful of beans over several layers of newspaper which are kept wet and soggy.

3 Place the beans in the bottom of a jar and several times a day add just enough water to keep them moist.

Bean sprouts can be served in a salad, as a garnish, or as a sandwich spread when chopped and mixed with salt and butter or margarine. With three jars or newspaper fields and a little planning any galley can become a ripe, sea-going farm.

Chapter 6

A Week at Sea

'I must be getting bored with my diet as I have cooked some crazy dishes recently – for example, spaghetti, peas, and curried prawns for supper this evening.'

Nigel Tetley, Trimaran Solo: 'Victress' round the World

'Ashore, coffee keeps me awake, but not here. And I sleep all I like during the day. People often imagine that sailors are a breed of supermen; that we almost never sleep, spend all our time handling sails, never get a hot meal. If they only knew!'

Bernard Moitessier, Long Way

NOTES FOR THE COOK

FOOD FOR: 21 meals, 1 birthday, 2 barbecues, 3 parties, 7 snacks. Daily cocktails at sunset. 1 Landfall celebration. Grog for the dogwatch.

CREW: Herman - a gourmet, likes soufflés, Stroganoffs & French coffee - full of advice - good Captain, but a bad cook. Mac - overweight, incipient glutton - no help in the galley - prone to seasickness and can-opener accidents. Susan - on a diet - hates garlic and onions - allergic to shellfish and Herman. Karen - drinks like a fish and only nibbles - prefers beer goulash and rum balls - often constipated. Amy - chocoholic - eats her weight every day - must lock up all sweets. Me - eat and drink anything, any time.

TO BUY: one prize for the best dishwasher - 4 scented candles - 3 cassettes of sunset music: Liszt, Bizet & Wagner - 2 rat traps.

TO CHECK: deck stereo speakers - game locker - charts for best barbecue beaches.

Beer Soup Two

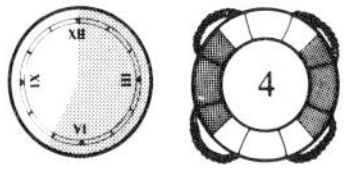

6 onions, sliced
2 tablespoons butter or margarine
3 cubes chicken bouillon
3 cups dark beer (brown ale)
½ teaspoon pepper
1 tablespoon flour
pinch of salt

Cook the onions and butter in a deep pan for about five minutes or until onions are soft. Add the flour, salt and pepper. Pour in the beer and the bouillon and simmer for about half an hour. Serve hot with toast.

Yellow Cheese Soup

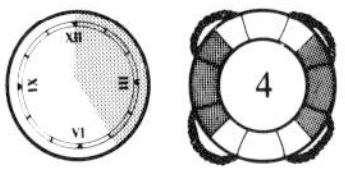

½ pound grated cheese, preferably Cheddar
2 tablespoons onions, chopped
2 tablespoons carrots, chopped
3 tablespoons green peppers, chopped
2 tablespoons butter or margarine
2 tablespoons flour
3 cups chicken bouillon
1 cup milk
salt and white pepper

Put butter into a large pot and simmer the vegetables until they are soft. Add the flour and bouillon, mix well, cover and let cook for about 10 minutes. Add cheese and milk – more may be necessary if the soup is too thick – season, and stir constantly until all the cheese has melted. Serve hot.

Apple-Cabbage Salad

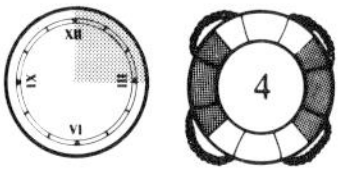

½ head cabbage, chopped
2 apples, peeled and chopped
1 tablespoon lemon juice
2 tablespoons cooking oil
1 tablespoon vinegar
pinch of caraway seeds or tarragon
1 teaspoon sugar

Mix cooking oil, vinegar, tarragon and sugar into a sauce. Use lemon juice to rub on apples, which prevents them from turning brown. Then pour sauce over cabbage and apples. Chill, if possible, and serve.

Margarita's Egg Salad

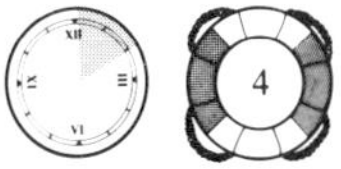

4 hard-boiled eggs
4 tablespoons mayonnaise
1 tablespoon olive oil
1 tablespoon ketchup (catsup)
1 palmful parsley
salt and pepper

Cut the eggs into small pieces, then add mayonnaise, olive oil and ketchup (catsup). Mix well, and season to taste. Before serving sprinkle on parsley.

Basic Fish Casserole

2–3 cups fish, any kind
1 cup condensed milk
1 onion, chopped
3 hard-boiled eggs, chopped
1 handful breadcrumbs
1 teaspoon mustard
1 tablespoon cooking oil
salt and pepper

Mix all ingredients except the breadcrumbs and butter, and pour them into a greased baking pan. Mix breadcrumbs and butter and sprinkle over the top. Bake in a moderate oven for about 30–45 minutes.

Variations:

1. Add Parmesan cheese to the breadcrumb and butter mix.
2. Add one pound of cooked noodles.
3. Flavour with a teaspoon of oregano.

Fishburgers

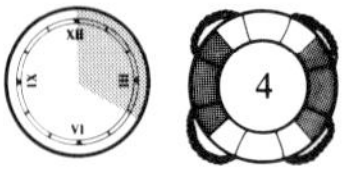

2–3 pounds fish fillets
1 pound cooked potatoes
juice of 1 lemon
3–4 tablespoons cooking oil
1 egg
salt and pepper

Mash potatoes, beat egg, mince fish, and combine with salt, pepper and cooking oil. When thoroughly mixed, shape into hamburger-like patties and fry in a hot pan.

Tunafish Spaghetti Sauce

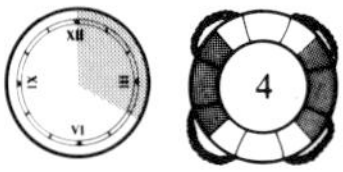

1 small can tuna, or 2 cooked fillets, chopped in pieces
1 small can mushrooms
½ cup olive oil
5 garlic cloves, crushed
1 palmful chopped parsley
1 medium can peeled tomatoes
1 can tomato purée (paste)
½ cup white wine
pinch of basil
salt and pepper

Sauté the garlic in olive oil, then add tomatoes and tomato purée (paste), basil, salt and pepper and tuna. Cook for about 10 minutes, adding wine to get a proper consistency to the sauce. Pour over hot spaghetti and sprinkle on parsley.

Kartoffelpuffer (German potato pancakes)

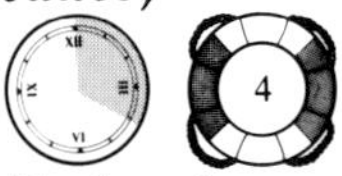

2 pounds of large potatoes
1 large onion
2–3 eggs, beaten
3 tablespoons cooking oil
salt and pepper

Peel and grate the onion and potatoes. Add eggs and salt and pepper. Mix well. Form into thin patties and cook on a hot griddle like pancakes. The thinner the better. Serve crisp and brown.

Eggs and Onions

3 pounds onions
6 eggs
½ can condensed milk
½ pound cheese, grated
4 tablespoons cooking oil
3 teaspoons salt
1 teaspoon paprika
dash of Tabasco sauce
pinch of pepper

Sauté the onions in oil, and add salt and pepper. In a bowl mix eggs, milk, cheese and paprika. Place the onions at the bottom of a large baking dish, then pour in the egg mixture. Bake in a moderate oven for half an hour.

Bacon and Banana Rice

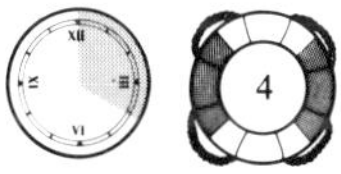

½ pound rice
½ pound bacon
½ stick (2 oz) butter or margarine
4 bananas cut lengthwise in halves
juice of ½ a lemon

Cook the rice and dry it completely. In a large saucepan fry the bacon in butter. Add the rice and mix thoroughly. In another pan fry the bananas. Add the lemon juice, then pour on top of the rice and serve.

Cauliflower Loaf

2 medium-sized cauliflowers, divided into pieces
1 tablespoon butter or margarine
3 pounds potatoes, cooked and cut in quarters
1 teaspoon salt
1 teaspoon white pepper
¼ teaspoon paprika
6 eggs
5 tablespoons cheese, grated

Put cauliflower in a large casserole, cover with water, add salt, and cook until soft – about 15 minutes. Dry the pieces, then place in a bowl and add butter, paprika, pepper, potatoes. Mix until a purée. Add the eggs, one by one, stirring constantly, and finally the cheese. Pour the mixture into a greased bread tin, cover and bake in a moderate oven for about 45 minutes.

Basic Biscuits

2 cups flour
3 teaspoons baking powder
$\frac{1}{4}$ cup cooking oil
1 cup milk
$\frac{1}{4}$ stick (1 oz) butter or margarine
pinch of salt

Mix all ingredients except the butter into a soft dough, then form into pats about a half inch thick. Place on an ungreased baking sheet and add a dollop of butter to the top of each pat. Bake in a hot oven for 15–20 minutes.

Basic Bread

6 cups flour
1 packet dry yeast
2 cups hot milk
2 tablespoons sugar
2 teaspoons salt
1 tablespoon shortening
$\frac{1}{4}$ cup warm water

Mix yeast in water and set to one side. In a large bowl mix the milk, sugar, salt, shortening and gradually add 2 cups of flour. When this has been dissolved, mix in the yeast, then any additional flour necessary to make a stiff dough. Cover, and let rise. When the dough has doubled, knead it down, and let it rise again. Mould the dough into two loaves, place in greased baking tins, and bake in a hot oven for about half an hour.

Variations:

1 Instead of shortening add 4–6 tablespoons of grated cheese.
2 Instead of forming the dough into loaves, roll into a rectangle and cut into rolls.

No-fail Dessert Dough

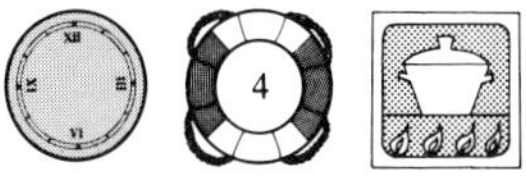

4 cups flour
1 cup scalded milk
$\frac{1}{4}$ cup sugar
1 teaspoon salt
1 packet dry yeast
1 beaten egg
$\frac{1}{4}$ cup warm water
$\frac{1}{2}$ stick (2 oz) butter or margarine

Mix yeast and water and set to one side. Combine milk, butter, sugar and salt, then add yeast, egg and half the flour in that order. When the mixture is smooth, add enough of the remaining flour to make a stiff dough. Then place it on a floured board and knead for several minutes. Cover, and let rise for an hour. Punch down, fashion into loaves or cakes, and bake in a hot oven for 30–40 minutes.

Variations:

1 Mould the dough into crescents and fill each with a tablespoonful of jam.
2 Use dates or chopped nuts as a filling.

Simple Frosting

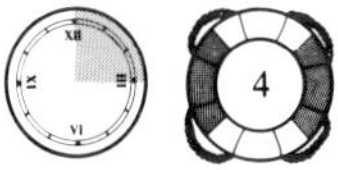

1 cup icing (confectioner's) sugar
$\frac{1}{4}$ cup milk
dash of vanilla essence (extract)
dash of lemon juice

Add just enough milk to the sugar to make a thick paste. Mix in the vanilla and lemon juice. When paste is completely smooth, spread on the cake.

Chapter 7

Heavy Weather

'At every heavy gust men, huddled together, whispered to one another: "It can blow no harder" – and presently the gale would give them the lie with a piercing shriek, and drive their breath back into their throats.'

Joseph Conrad, The Nigger of the 'Narcissus'

'The whole sea . . . was lashed into ingovernable fury . . . the vast bed of waters, seamed and scarred into a thousand conflicting channels, burst suddenly into frenzied convulsion – heaving, boiling, hissing – gyrating in gigantic and innumerable vortices, and all whirling and plunging on to the eastward with a rapidity which water never elsewhere assumes, except in precipitous descents.'

Edgar Allan Poe, A Descent into the Maelström

'The next night was still worse; the seas grew higher instead of going down . . . and the seas got the better of us and hurled us round and sideways, while the water poured on board. Then we changed over to one hour at the helm and an hour and a half's rest. So the first sixty hours passed, in one continuous struggle against a chaos of waves that rushed upon us, one after another, without cessation. High waves and low waves, pointed waves and round waves, slanting waves and waves on the top of other waves.'

Thor Heyerdahl, Kon-Tiki Expedition

The seas are steep, confused and tipped with foam. Each time the bow cuts into a wave spray slaps over the windward rail and lashes your face. No matter which way you twist, the wind still whips through your oilskins and a stream of icy water trickles down your back.

The storm goes on, with no end in sight. Shivering, you grip the spokes of the wheel and try to hold the boat on course. Your watch has become a lonely, cold vigil.

Then the hatch opens, and with a friendly wave a bowl is thrust towards you. Balancing it between your knees, you spoon warmth into your body. Once again the Cook has performed a miracle.

Pressure Cookers

No galley should be without one for they are so practical it seems they were invented by a sea-going chef. Actually, a 17th-century French physicist, Denis Papin, who had no interest in boats whatsoever, built the first one. In any case a pressure cooker is the Cook's genie. It cuts cooking time by as much as two-thirds, saves fuel, helps retain vitamins and minerals, bakes bread in 20 minutes, and can turn a one burner stove into a whole range. What's more, food cooked in a pressure cooker and left sealed will keep for nearly a week.

Tinned Food

For a weekend cruise or an Atlantic crossing tinned food is nearly always a staple. Before stocking the boat be sure to check the quality and canning dates, and remember that tins are a potential hazard. Nothing can block a bilge pump faster than a few gummy labels.

It is best to remove the labels before storing. One easy method is to paste a label in the food logbook, give it a number, and paint it on the top of the tins. Then varnish them and store in the bilge. When a tin is used it can be marked off in the logbook, thus providing an almost instant assessment of the stores. Check the tins periodically as the boat's movement may wear off some of the varnish.

Storm Food

Force 6–7: Stews, goulashes, thick soups, chilli and puddings
Force 8–9: Simple one-pot meals, muesli and hash
Force 10–11: Chocolate bars, raisins, dried fruit, nuts and tinned food which can be eaten cold from the tin
Force 12 plus: Wafers

Gulf Stream Pea Soup

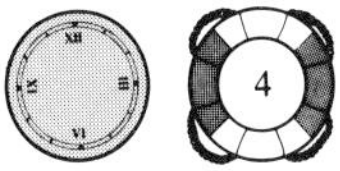

1 pound potatoes, peeled and diced
1 small can corned beef
1 medium can peas
salt and pepper

Boil the potatoes, drain them, then add the can of peas, its liquid and the corned beef. Mix well, and season to taste. If the soup is too thick, thin with water. Simmer for at least an hour.

Simple Borsch

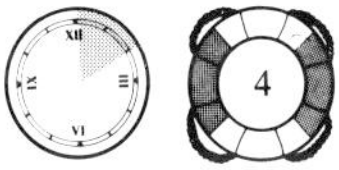

1 jar beetroot, diced
1 large can beef soup
2 tablespoons lemon juice
handful of chopped chives or parsley

Mix the soup and beetroot. Add the lemon juice and chill if possible. Sprinkle on the chives just before serving.

Typhoon Soup

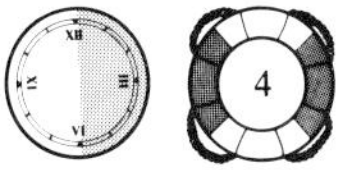

1 pound stewing meat
1 small can mixed vegetables
2 onions, chopped
1 potato, peeled and chopped
¼ stick (1 oz) butter or margarine
salt and pepper

Heat the butter in a casserole and fry the onions and meat. Add the juice from the can of vegetables, then the potatoes. Simmer for 20 minutes. Add water, if necessary. Stir in the mixed vegetables and season to taste.

Irish Stew

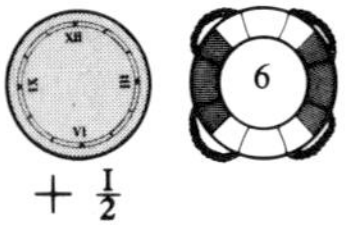

2 pounds mutton, chopped into small pieces
3 pounds potatoes, peeled and quartered
8 onions, quartered
1 quart bouillon
salt and pepper

Put half the potatoes and onions in a pot and cover with a layer of meat. Then add the rest of the potatoes and onions and another layer of meat. Pour in just enough bouillon to cover the meat and cook for about an hour and a half.

Bauernfrühstück (Farmer's breakfast)

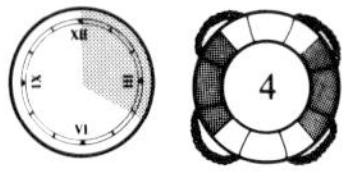

4 eggs
4–6 rashers (slices) bacon
1 onion, chopped
4 boiled potatoes, chopped
salt and pepper

Cook the bacon until crisp, then remove from pan. Add the onion and potato. When brown, crumble in the bacon. Beat the eggs and pour over the mixture. Cook as if it were an omelette.

Mistral Muesli

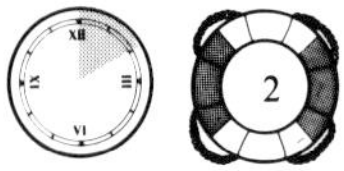

¼ cup oatmeal
1 cup milk
1 apple, peeled and grated
1 banana, sliced
1 teaspoon lemon juice
2 tablespoons raisins
3 tablespoons chopped nuts

Soak the oatmeal in milk for about 10 minutes, then add the rest of the ingredients and mix.

Beer Goulash

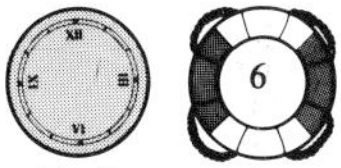

× 2

3 pounds stewing meat
2 pounds onions
2 small cans tomato purée (paste)
2 medium cans beer
2 bay leaves
pinch of paprika
salt and pepper

Cut the meat into cubes and brown in a frying pan. Then transfer to a large casserole and add sliced onions, bay leaves, beer, salt and pepper, and paprika. Mix in the tomato purée (paste), cover the pot and cook for several hours, or until the meat is tender.

Santiago's Chilli

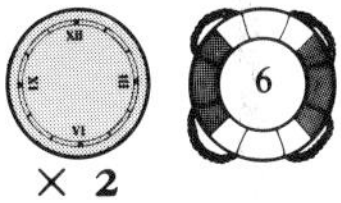

× 2

3 pounds chopped steak, minced (hamburger) meat or stewing meat
2 medium cans beef soup
4–6 teaspoons chilli powder
3–5 garlic cloves, crushed
1 teaspoon oregano
6 tablespoons flour
5 tablespoons cooking oil
salt

Put cooking oil into a deep frying pan, add meat and brown. Add chilli powder and flour, then salt, oregano, soup and garlic. Simmer over a low flame for hours. The longer, the better.

Starboard Hash

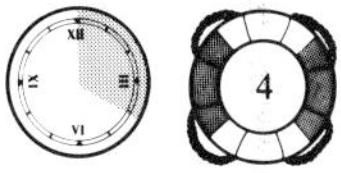

1 small can corned beef
4 large boiled potatoes
2 eggs
2 tablespoons butter or margarine
palmful of flour
salt and pepper

Mash the potatoes and mix in the eggs. Add salt and pepper, then the corned beef which has been chopped into small chunks. Roll into balls about an inch in diameter and dust with flour. Fry in hot butter until brown.

Hungarian Goulash

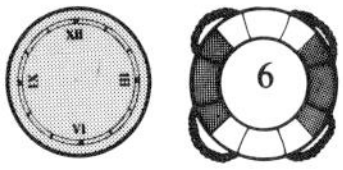

3 pounds stewing meat
2 pounds onions, quartered
1 small can tomato purée (paste)
2 medium cans beer
¼ cup cooking oil
2 bay leaves
pinch of paprika
salt and pepper

Put oil in a frying pan and brown the meat, then transfer it to a large casserole. Add onions and bay leaves, and cook slowly for about 10 minutes. Pour in the beer and tomato purée (paste) and bring to the boil. Season with salt, pepper and paprika and simmer for several hours.

Orion Cornbread

¼ pound cornmeal
1 cup milk
3 eggs, separated
2 tablespoons butter or margarine
pinch of salt

Heat milk in a large pot, stir slowly and gradually mix in the cornmeal. Do not boil. Add salt and butter and turn off the flame. Mix in the egg yolks, one at a time, then the egg whites which have been stiffly beaten. Pour the dough into a greased baking tin and bake in a moderate oven for about 30 minutes.

Captain Bligh's Bread Pudding

6 slices buttered stale bread
2 fingers rum
2 cups milk
½ cup sugar
4 eggs
dash of vanilla essence (extract)

Quarter the bread, then use pieces to line a medium-sized baking dish. Mix milk, sugar, vanilla essence (extract) and rum in a small pot, and heat until the milk scalds. Beat the eggs in a bowl, then pour into the cooled milk. Mix thoroughly. Pour mixture into the baking dish and bake in a moderate oven for about half an hour.

Keeping Things Dry

Rice makes an excellent desiccant to help keep tape recorders, photo equipment and electronic gear free of moisture. Spread a handful of rice over the bottom of a clean, dry frying pan, and heat it until it becomes brown. Then put it in a cheesecloth bag and store it inside the equipment. When the rice becomes moist, throw it away and repeat the process.

Chapter 8

Feeding the Sick

'Happiness for me is largely a matter of digestion.'

Lin Yutang

'. . . our black cook; who according to the invariable custom at sea, always went by the name of the doctor.

And doctors, *cooks certainly are; the very best medicos in the world . . .'*

Herman Melville, Redburn

'Then he told us anecdotes of how he had gone across the Channel when it was so rough that the passengers had to be tied into their berths, and he and the captain were the only two living souls on board who were not ill. Sometimes it was he and the second mate who were not ill; but it was generally he and one other man. If not he and another man, then it was he by himself.'

Jerome K. Jerome, Three Men in a Boat

His body bent over the rail, face in the wake, the sea-sick sailor is a pitiful sight. Weak, pallid and helpless, he has forgotten about seamanship and navigation. His spirits have fallen to the pit of his stomach and each undulating wave only makes him a little greener. Convinced he is going to die, with his last ounce of strength he lashes himself to the mast and awaits the end.

Only the Cook can save him. The galley becomes a pharmacy for porridge, teas, soups and pudding. With simple nourishment and a little gentle insistence, cup by cup, the Cook nurses the sailor back to life.

A Few Facts About Sea-sickness

Nine out of ten people are likely to become sea-sick.

Those most susceptible are: women, children between 2 and 10, the thin, the anaemic, the nervous and the over-weight.

Those nearly immune are: the old, the very young and the deaf.

The cause: The motion of the boat disturbs the normal equilibrium of the inner ear, producing a sensation of instability. This is intensified by the visual perception of movement and the irritation of food rolling in the digestive tract. Another important factor is expectation, the psychological fear of becoming sick which creates its own self-fulfilling prophecy.

The symptoms: headache, a cold sweat, a feeling of weakness and apathy, vomiting, and in extreme cases, depression to the point of suicide.

The remedy: A number of anti-sea-sickness drugs are on the market, and all have been proved effective. But since vomiting is nearly always a problem, those in suppository form are the most useful.

However, the equilibrium of the inner ear can be trained. A few exercises, done morning and evening, several days before a voyage can be surprisingly helpful. Stand with your feet wide apart and sway your body in a circular motion for 5–10 minutes. Also practise rolling your eyes in imitation of the motion of a boat. If this produces a slight nausea, stop until it passes, then continue.

If you do become sea-sick:
Don't go below. Stay in the fresh air.
Keep warm and dry.
Avoid the sun.
Drink very little.
Eat small amounts of soft food every few hours.
Close your eyes or focus only on the horizon.

Sick-bay Soup

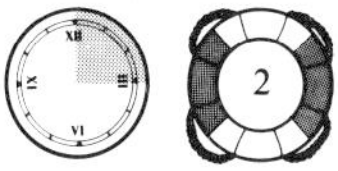

3 cups milk
3 tablespoons oatmeal
2 tablespoons sugar
knob of butter
pinch of salt

Heat the milk. When it boils add the oatmeal. Stir, and let simmer for about 10 minutes. Add salt and sugar, and before serving, the knob of butter.

Milky Way Rice

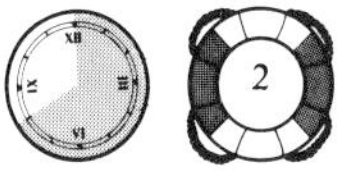

1 quart milk
1 cup rice
4 tablespoons sugar
twist of lemon peel
pinch of salt
a few drops vanilla essence (extract)

Mix the milk, rice, salt and lemon twist in a large casserole and set aside for half an hour. Then cook over a low flame, stirring often, until the rice becomes soft. Mix in vanilla essence (extract), sprinkle on sugar and serve, either hot or cold.

Blue Nose Pancakes

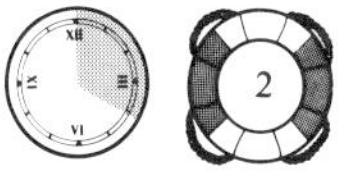

1 can corn
3 eggs, separated
1 teaspoon flour
2 tablespoons butter or margarine
salt and pepper

In a bowl, mix the egg yolks, flour, salt, pepper and corn without its liquid. Beat the egg whites until they are stiff, then fold into the mixture. Heat butter in a frying pan until it steams, then cook the batter like pancakes.

Black Spot Bread

1 egg
1 cup milk
1 cup cornmeal
1 cup cold boiled rice
½ cup flour
3 teaspoons baking powder
palmful of raisins
pinch of salt

Beat the egg, then add salt, cornmeal, rice, raisins and milk. Mix well, and stir in the flour and baking powder. When the mixture is the consistency of dough – a little water may have to be added – place in a greased baking pan and bake in a moderate oven for half an hour.

Wrecked Eggs on a Potato Beach

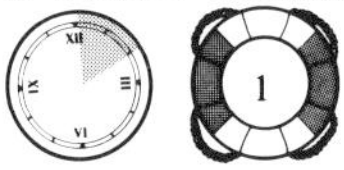

2 eggs, poached
2 potatoes, boiled
2 tablespoons milk
2–4 tablespoons grated cheese

Mix milk and potatoes and beat into a purée. Place the eggs on top and cover with cheese.

French Toast Sandwich

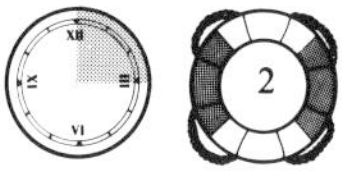

sliced ham and/or cheese
2 eggs, beaten
1 tablespoon sugar
4 slices bread
2 tablespoons butter or margarine
salt and pepper

Put eggs in a bowl, add sugar, salt and pepper. Dip bread into the batter, turning it with a spatula. Heat butter in a frying pan, and fry soaked bread until brown. Serve as a sandwich with sliced ham and/or cheese.

Saragossa Omelette

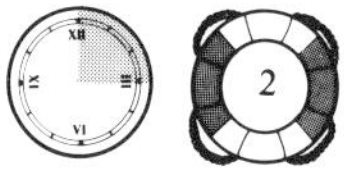

1 medium can mixed vegetables
4 eggs
2 tablespoons butter or margarine
1 onion, sliced
pinch of basil
salt and pepper

Fry the onion in butter until brown. After draining the mixed vegetables, pour into the pan and season with salt, pepper and basil. Add the eggs, mix well and cook on both sides.

Rice Soufflé

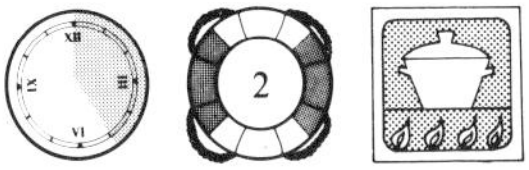

½ pound cooked rice
1½ cups milk
3 tablespoons sugar
1 teaspoon lemon juice
½ stick (2 oz) butter or margarine
4 egg yolks
palmful of raisins

Combine rice, raisins, sugar, lemon juice and all except one tablespoon of milk. Mix well, then pour into a greased baking dish. Add egg yolks to the remainder of the milk and pour over the rice. Slice butter into pats, lay on top and bake in a hot oven for 10–15 minutes.

Cunji Water

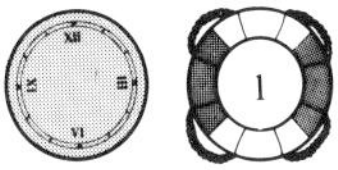

3 tablespoons rice
1 teaspoon lime juice
2 cups water
pinch of salt

Simmer the rice in the water for about an hour, then strain off the liquid and let it cool. Add the salt and lime juice and serve.

Albumin Water

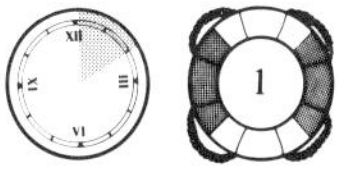

4 egg whites
juice of ½ a lemon
1 cup water
1 teaspoon sugar

Beat the egg whites, then add the water, lemon juice and sugar. Let stand for a few minutes until everything is dissolved, then serve.

St. Elmo's Fire

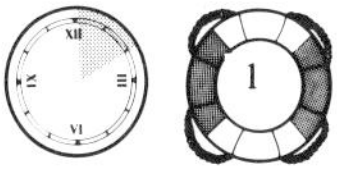

3 egg yolks
1 cup hot milk
2 slices bread
pinch of nutmeg

Mix the egg yolks and nutmeg, then add milk and beat well. Place the bread in a bowl and pour the mixture over it.

Sick Sailor's Grog

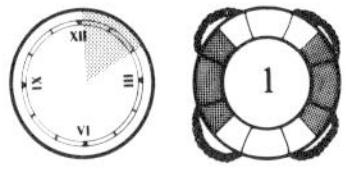

2 fingers light rum
1 cup hot milk
1 tablespoon honey
1 clove

Heat the milk and rum together so that most of the alcohol burns off, then add the clove and honey.

Constipation and Diarrhoea

Constipation is usually caused by a change in diet or environment, hence it often accompanies the beginning of a voyage. However, it should not be regarded as a serious problem. Two or three days without a bowel movement will not do the body any harm. Plenty of fluids – preferably hot – fresh fruit, vegetables and exercise should provide the solution. If not, then try a laxative.

Diarrhoea, on the other hand, can be a more serious matter. The two common causes are: (1) consuming bad food or drink, such as unripe or over-ripe fruit, bad tinned foods, inferior wine or beer, or impure water; and (2) food contaminated by bacteria, such as that badly cleaned or prepared, kept too long or left in reach of flies or other insects.

Treatment: no food, sufficient liquid to prevent dehydration and no exercise. If recovery does not start within 24 hours, put into port for medical attention.

Burns

In cases where there is no burn ointment on board the galley can serve as a medicine chest.

To stop pain and help prevent blisters, coat the burned area completely with the white of an egg or with plain bar of soap dissolved in a little water.

A paste made from salt and a few drops of water will also prevent blisters from forming.

Should blisters appear, they should be punctured with a sterilized needle, drained and kept clean.

The pain of a burned mouth can be lessened by slowly drinking some cream or by sucking on some butter.

Poisoned Fish

Unfortunately, in tropical waters the threat of fish poisoning is real. Just about any fish worth eating *can* be poisoned – mullet, eel, herring, shark, turtle and shellfish. And, to make matters worse, there is no way of knowing beforehand whether or not a fish is contaminated.

One thing is clear – the phenomenon is regional, to such an extent that fish on one side of a lagoon or bay can be poisoned and on the other side completely healthy.

Obviously, the best means of protection is local knowledge. In the absence of that, here are a few general rules:

1 Do not eat the viscera – heart, liver, etc.

2 Eat smaller varieties of fish, those of less than a kilo.

3 Soak the cleaned, filleted fish in water for at least an hour, changing the water several times.

In the event someone does become poisoned, induce vomiting, and then, of course, find a local doctor as soon as possible.

Scurvy

Until the connection between a vitamin C deficiency and scurvy was discovered in the 18th century, the disease was the sourge of mariners. And surprisingly, even today many yachtsmen develop mild cases of it, often without realizing it.

The symptons can be rather confusing, especially in the early states, and very idiosyncratic. During Anson's voyage around the world 626 of his crew of 961 died from scurvy. He wrote:

> Its symptoms are inconstant and innumerable, and its progress and effects extremely irregular; for scarcely two persons have complaints exactly resembling each other, and where there hath been found some conformity in the symptoms, the order of their appearance has been totally different.

In general, the early phases of scurvy are marked by listlessness, fatigue, a lack of endurance, shortness of breath and aches and pains in the joints or muscles, particularly at night. Later, gums begin to bleed, haemorrhages occur in the muscles and joints, scars break open and wounds refuse to heal.

The cure, of course, is vitamin C – about 500 mg. daily – and recuperation is dramatically rapid. Although limes are the traditional preventative on long passages, lemons have substantially more anti-scorbutic value. Apparently the mistake arose from the fact that West Indians called a lemon a lime.

Honey as Medicine

Honey is a source of instant energy and thus an essential item in the ship's larder. Ordinary sugar must be digested by the body before it can produce energy, but honey sugar has been 'predigested' in the bee's honey stomach, and hence goes to work almost immediately. It is therefore an excellent food for people suffering from digestive problems.

For a sore throat, a soothing gargle can be prepared from a warm mixture of honey and water. And when a crisis arises, a teaspoon of honey taken several times a day is said to have a calming, sedative effect.

In emergencies, honey can be applied to burns and wounds as

it stops bleeding, keeps the air away from the skin, helps to lessen pain and prevents blisters from forming. Also, mixed with glycerine, it makes an excellent lotion for chapped or rough skin.

If stored in a cool place, honey will remain fresh even for the longest passage. Should it crystallize, it can be re-liquified by warming it in a pan of hot water.

Sea Water as Medicine

A couple of fingers of sea water, diluted with two or three times as much fresh water, makes an excellent morning tonic. Besides helping to keep body functions regular, it also will supply you with many essential minerals such as sodium, magnesium, calcium and potassium.

Potato Juice

Potatoes, a staple on almost every yacht, are a source of vitamin C, B1, B2 and B6. However, these vitamins are lost when potatoes are cooked.

To get a high nutritive value, dice and squeeze about ½ pound of raw potatoes. Drink the juice immediately. It may not taste good, but it will provide you with the minimum daily requirements of these vitamins. This drink can also be used to relieve stomach cramps or acid indigestion.

Chapter 9

The Unforgettable Moment

'Bad cooks – and the utter lack of reason in the kitchen – have delayed human development longest and impaired it most.'

Nietzsche, Beyond Good and Evil

'The discovery of a new dish does more for the happiness of the human race than the discovery of a star.'

Brillat-Savarin, Physiologie du Goût

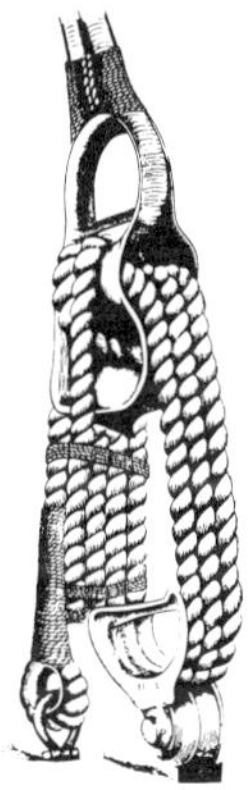

Beginning with the maiden voyage, sailing is full of important events: passing the breakwater, crossing the Channel or the Tropic of Capricorn, losing a race or a mast, raising the spinnaker, putting down a mutiny or just a lovely day tied up in the marina.

All deserve a celebration and the Cook is always the Master of Ceremonies.

After the Race

Royal Beef Stroganoff

$1\frac{1}{2}$ pounds sirloin, cut into thin strips
1 small can mushrooms
1 cup sour cream
1 onion, sliced
2 garlic cloves, crushed
1 medium can beef soup
1 handful breadcrumbs
2 tablespoons butter or margarine
salt and pepper

Sauté the onion and garlic in butter. Salt and pepper the breadcrumbs, then coat the meat. Add to the frying pan and brown on both sides. Mix in the soup and let simmer for half an hour. Just before serving add the mushrooms and fold in the sour cream.

Poseidon's Rum Pancakes

6–8 pancakes – see recipe for Basic Pancakes (p. 44)
$\frac{1}{4}$ pound almonds, chopped
4 eggs
4 tablespoons sugar
2 fingers rum
$\frac{1}{3}$ ($1\frac{1}{2}$ oz) stick butter
dash of lemon juice

Beat half the butter, the sugar and egg yolks until foamy. Add rum, almonds and lemon juice. Cut the pancakes into thin slices and fold them into the mixture. Pour into a casserole greased with the rest of the butter and bake in a moderate oven for half an hour.

Passing the Lighthouse

Drunken Onions

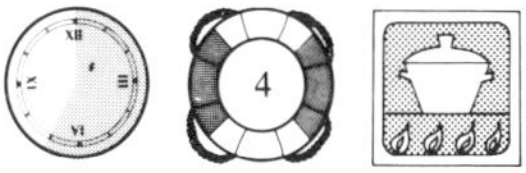

6 large onions, peeled
2 glasses wine, red or white
1 tablespoon olive oil
1 glass water

Place the onions in a baking dish with the olive oil and heat on top of the stove. When the oil is hot, pour in the wine, then just enough water so that the liquid half covers the onions. Bake in a low oven for half an hour.

Blue Peter Salad

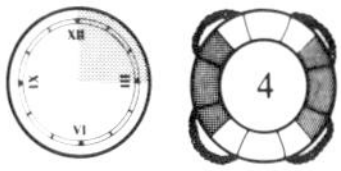

1 cabbage, chopped
1 teaspoon sugar
2 carrots, chopped
2 pineapple rings, chopped
½ cup ham, diced
1 teaspoon dry mustard
1 tablespoon vinegar
½ teaspoon salt
pinch of black pepper

Combine cabbage, carrots, pineapple and ham in a salad bowl. Then mix mustard, salt, pepper, sugar and vinegar into a sauce.

Leeward Liver

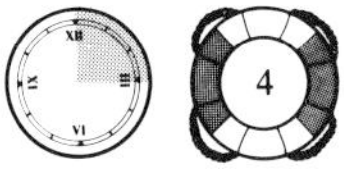

4 thick slices liver
½ stick (2 oz) butter
2 tablespoons flour
½ glass sherry or white wine
½ tablespoon salt
pinch of white pepper

Melt the butter in a frying pan, and before it browns add the liver which has been coated in flour. When cooked remove from pan. Add salt, pepper and sherry or wine to the remaining butter. Bring to the boil and pour over the liver.

Baked Apples

4 large apples, cored
⅓ pound sugar
2 cups boiling water
1 palmful raisins
1 palmful chopped nuts
pinch of cinnamon

Place the apples in a buttered baking dish and fill the cores with nuts and raisins. Mix sugar, water and cinnamon in a pot and heat for 8–10 minutes. Pour over the apples, then bake them in a low oven for at least half an hour.

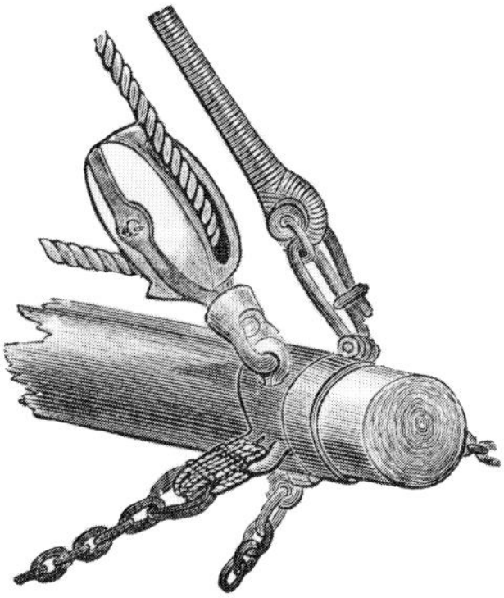

Rescue

The Ancient Mariner's Omelette

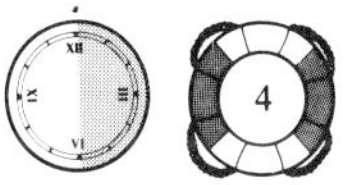

8 eggs
4 tomatoes, sliced
1 onion, sliced
1 garlic clove, crushed
1 green pepper, sliced
2 tablespoons olive oil
3 tablespoons beef bouillon
2 tablespoons condensed milk
$\frac{1}{3}$ stick ($1\frac{1}{2}$ oz) butter
8 stoned (pitted) black olives
2 palmfuls chopped parsley
salt and pepper

Heat the oil in a saucepan, then add green pepper, tomatoes, bouillon and salt and pepper. Beat the eggs in a bowl with the milk and half the parsley. Pour into a buttered frying pan and cook the omelette. When ready, pour over the sauce and garnish the olives and parsley.

Garlic Toast

8 slices bread
3 tablespoons olive oil
5 garlic cloves, crushed

Mix the garlic and olive oil, then paint on both sides of the bread. Toast until brown.

A Birthday

Sweet and Sour Salad

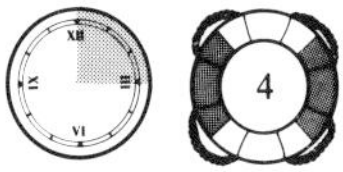

2 cucumbers, sliced, or 1 cabbage, sliced
½ cup wine vinegar
½ cup water
1 tablespoon sugar
¼ cup salad oil
handful of chopped onions
handful of chopped parsley
salt and pepper

Place the sliced cabbage or cucumbers in a bowl. Mix the other ingredients into a sauce and add to the bowl. If possible, let stand for several hours before serving.

Jubilee Pepper Steak

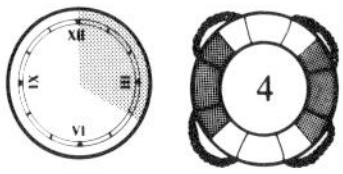

4 thick steaks
4 fingers cognac
4 teaspoons black pepper
2 teaspoons cooking oil
1 stick (¼ lb) butter or margarine
8 tablespoons condensed milk
1 teaspoon mustard powder

Paint the steaks with oil and pepper both sides. Melt the butter in a frying pan and when hot add the steaks. Cook to taste, flambé with cognac and remove from pan. Stir in the milk and mustard to the remaining butter, then pour the sauce over the steaks.

Crêpes Marins

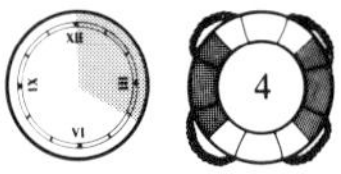

2 cups flour
4 eggs
1 cup milk
1 cup water
4 tablespoons melted butter
pinch of salt

Mix the flour, eggs and salt, then add the milk, water and butter. Stir until the batter is smooth. If possible, set aside for several hours in a cool place before using. Cook in a hot skillet coated with oil. When pouring in the batter, tilt the pan in all directions so that the crêpe is as thin as possible. Cook for about half a minute on one side, then flip to the other. Crêpes can be served with butter, jams, cinnamon and sugar, and flambéd in rum or cognac.

Meeting the Marie Celeste

Blood Soup

2 cups red wine
2 tablespoons rice
3 tablespoons sugar
2 cloves
pinch of cinnamon

Boil $1\frac{1}{2}$ cups of water, then add cinnamon, cloves and rice. Mix well, and let simmer for 15 minutes. When rice is soft, add the wine and sugar. Heat, but do not boil. Serve hot.

Atlantis Soufflé

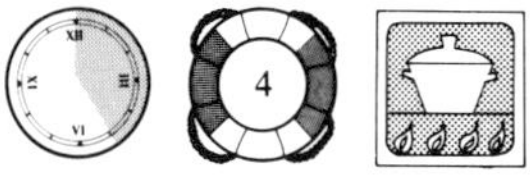

6 eggs, separated
4 tablespoons butter
$\frac{3}{4}$–1 cup filling: grated cheese, chopped meat or fish
1 teaspoon salt
pinch of pepper

Add the salt to the egg whites and beat until stiff. Place the yolks in another bowl, and beat well. Add pepper, then gradually fold in the whites. Do not mix too thoroughly. Heat butter in a frying pan until brown, then add the eggs and filling. After a minute or two, move the frying pan into a moderate oven, and bake for 5–10 minutes. Serve immediately.

Bananas Amontillado

8 bananas, peeled and cut lengthwise
4 tablespoons butter
3 tablespoons honey
3 fingers sherry
juice of 1 lemon

Grease a baking pan with butter, add the bananas, then pour the lemon juice over them. Mix honey, sherry and the rest of the butter, and pour sauce over the bananas. Cook in a slow oven for 20 minutes, and baste the bananas with the sauce.

'Interview' with the Cook of the Marie Celeste

Interviewer: Could you please tell us, in your own words, what really happened on board the *Marie Celeste*.

Cook: Well, first of all, contrary to what they say, she wasn't deserted when they found her. I was on board. The accident was my fault, I suppose.

You see, that morning I made a favourite sauce of mine, Limburger purée, and I neglected to warn the crew. The smell got to be a bit overpowering, I guess. Anyway, they all took to the long boat, paid out some line, and drifted astern to wait for the ship to air out. Then the line parted and that was the last I ever saw of them.

'Interview' with the Cook of the **Intrepid**

Interviewer: Could you please tell us, in your own words, why did the *Intrepid* lose the race?

Cook: Well, I suppose it was my fault. I started preparing the Bouillabaise as we rounded the last buoy. We were way ahead, and when the soup was ready I called the crew down to the galley. I really don't know what happened after that, except that when we went back up on deck we were sailing in somebody's wake. But on one point everyone's agreed. That was the most fantastic Bouillabaise I've ever made.

Chapter 10

On the Beach

'. . . I was resolv'd to feast him the next day with roasting a piece of the kid; this I did by hanging it before the fire on a string, as I had seen many people do in England, setting two poles up, one on each side of the fire, and one cross the top, and tying the string to the cross-stick, letting the meat turn continually. This Friday admir'd very much; but when he came to taste the flesh, he took so many ways to tell me how well he lik'd it, that I could not but understand him; and at last he told me he would never eat man's flesh any more, which I was very glad to hear.'

Daniel Defoe, Robinson Crusoe

From the moment the lookout cries, 'Land Ho!' the atmosphere on board changes. The methodical sea-going routine is broken and everyone's mind wanders towards the tip of land jutting above the horizon.

The Captain's landfall is made; he breaks out a new set of charts and begins to worry about tides, currents, reefs and anchorages. The crew forgets about watches, work slows down and conversation turns to bars, mail, fresh fruit and native women.

But the instant the Cook sees the shore he collects his spices, sauces and grilling irons. He knows the crew hungers for the taste of charred meat and marinade, and for a barbecue he will have to move to the beach.

Fish Barbecue Sauce

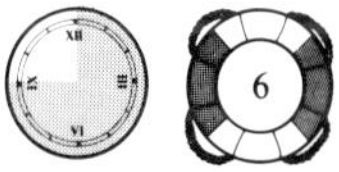

1 cup cooking wine
1 small can tomato purée
1 onion, chopped
2–4 garlic cloves, crushed
1 celery stalk, chopped
3 dashes Tabasco sauce
1 dash Worcestershire sauce
pinch of thyme and rosemary
salt and pepper

Heat slowly all the ingredients except the wine. Add it gradually to thin the sauce. Bring to the boil, then let simmer for at least half an hour before using. Can be served hot or cold.

Variations:

1 Use sherry instead of wine for a sweeter sauce.

2 Add more Tabasco sauce and/or chilli powder for a hot Mexican flavour.

3 Instead of Worcestershire sauce and Tabasco add more tomato purée, basil and oregano for an Italian taste.

Chimischurri

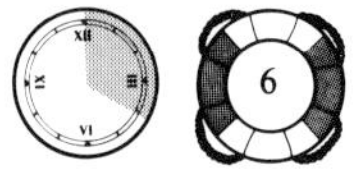

6 cloves of garlic, crushed
4 teaspoons cooking oil
$\frac{1}{2}$ cup vinegar
$\frac{1}{2}$ cup boiling water
1 teaspoon black pepper
6 teaspoons oregano
1 teaspoon cayenne pepper
1 teaspoon salt

Combine all the ingredients. Mix well, then pour into a bottle or jar. The sauce will keep almost indefinitely.

Barbecued Beerburgers

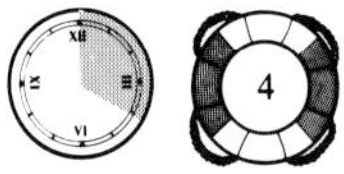

2 pounds minced (hamburger) beef
1 onion, chopped
1 green pepper, chopped
2 tablespoons butter or margarine
$\frac{1}{4}$ cup ketchup (catsup)
1 medium can beer
2 teaspoons cornflour (cornstarch)
1 dash of Worcestershire sauce

Place the butter in a frying pan and cook onion and green pepper until they are soft. Then add ketchup (catsup), Worcestershire sauce, cornflour (cornstarch) and beer. Bring the mixture to the boil, then let it simmer for at least 10 minutes. Make the meat into patties, and paint them continuously with the sauce as they grill.

Scupper Steak

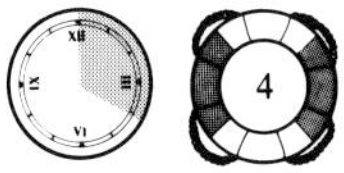

4 steaks, any cut
4 slices of ham
4 large bay leaves
3 tablespoons cooking oil
1 tablespoon tomato purée (paste)
pinch of basil
salt and pepper

Mix the oil, tomato purée (paste), salt, pepper and basil into a sauce, and marinate the steaks for several hours. Then smear both sides with the sauce, wrap with ham and bay leaves and grill to taste.

Steak Butter

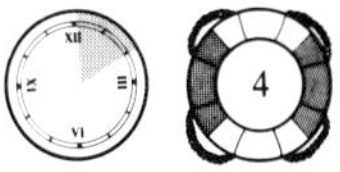

1 stick (¼ pound) butter or margarine
2 cloves garlic, crushed
2 tablespoons lemon juice
palmful of chopped parsley
dash of cayenne pepper or Tabasco sauce

Cream the butter with a fork, then slowly mix in the rest of the ingredients. Mould the butter into pats, and serve one for each steak.

Chef's Coleslaw

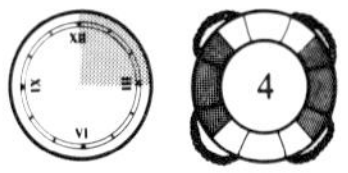

1 head of cabbage, sliced
1 cup sour cream
1 tablespoon sugar
1 tablespoon horseradish
1 teaspoon mustard powder
juice of 1 lemon
salt and pepper

Mix all the ingredients except the cabbage into a sauce. Use a little water if necessary to get the proper consistency. Pour over the cabbage and let stand for several hours before serving.

Vegetables on the Grill:

Onions

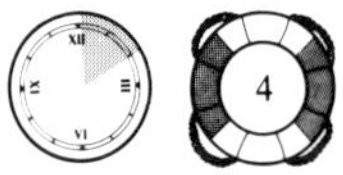

4 onions, peeled, and cut in thick slices
3 fingers whisky
dash of olive oil
salt and pepper

Pour a little whisky on each onion slice, add a drop or two of olive oil, salt and pepper, and grill immediately.

Tomatoes

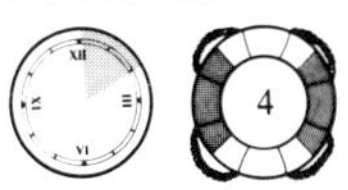

4 tomatoes, cut in halves
3 fingers gin
dash of olive oil
salt and pepper

Prepare in the same manner as the onions.

Jamaican Corn-on-the-Cob

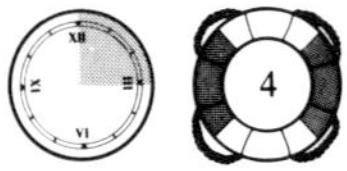

4 cobs (ears) of ripe corn
3 fingers rum
1 tablespoon sugar
2 tablespoons butter or margarine
salt and pepper

Mix all the ingredients except the corn into a sauce. Paint on the corn while it grills, and save enough for a last coat just before serving.

Grilled Fillet Catalan

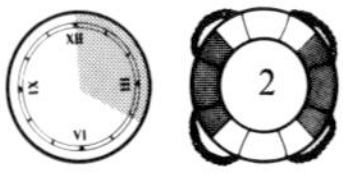

1 thick fillet
1 lemon, sliced
2–3 garlic cloves, crushed
¼ stick butter or margarine
pinch of salt
pinch of pepper

Place a piece of aluminium foil on the grill, turn up the edges and lay the fillet on a bed of lemon slices. Heat the butter and garlic, then pour it over the fish. Sprinkle with salt and pepper and cook slowly. Baste with the juice.

Marinade à l'Ariégeoise

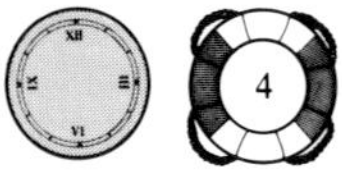

½ cup soya sauce
½ cup orange juice
4 tablespoons ketchup (catsup)
3–4 cloves garlic, crushed
juice of one lemon
pinch of pepper

Mix all the ingredients and marinate the fish for about an hour. Cook on a hot grill and baste with the marinade.

Banana Dog

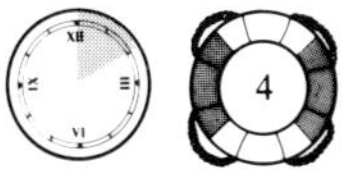

4 bananas, peeled
4 slices of ham
4 slices of cheese
2 tablespoons cooking oil
pinch of curry powder

Smear the bananas with oil and grill them lightly on both sides.

Sprinkle the ham with curry powder, then wrap a slice, and one of cheese, around each banana. Tie with a toothpick and grill again.

Sangria Punch

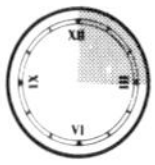

1 lemon, sliced
1 apple, sliced
1 orange, sliced
½ pound sugar
2 bottles dry red wine
½ cup cognac
1 bottle soda water

In a large crock or punch bowl combine all the fruit and half the sugar. Add the wine and cognac, then stir in the rest of the sugar. Let stand for about an hour, then add soda water and serve as cool as possible.

Grilled Fish

Lightly flour the fish or fillet, paint it with cooking oil, then place it on a well-oiled grill. Steaks and fillets will require more oil than a whole fish with the skin still on. Brush on more oil as the fish cooks and allow about 10 minutes on a hot grill for each inch of thickness.

Chapter 11

The Cook as Peacemaker

'Galley! . . . my business!' he shouted.

'Cook's going crazy now,' said several voices.

He yelled: 'Crazy, am I? I am more ready to die than any of you, officers incloosive – there! As long as she swims I will cook! I will get you coffee.'

'Cook, ye are a gentleman!' cried Belfast.

Joseph Conrad, The Nigger of the 'Narcissus'

'Spread the table and contention will cease.' English proverb

A ship at sea can be a floating paradise, buoyed up by friendship and enthusiasm, or at times, unfortunately, a prison of volatile emotions. When tempers flare between crew members, no bowsprit is long enough, no mast tall enough or no bilge deep enough to escape from the conflict. Suddenly, the whole ship seethes with hate, and who knows what direction it will turn – to violence, bloodshed or even mutiny?

As always, the Cook is in command. His recipe is simple and traditional.

He summons the crew to the galley, serves a strong grog, then an extravagant meal with special delicacies for everyone. When stomachs are full and passions weakened, the Cook lays his rolling pin and spoon on the table and announces the galley closed until the argument is settled.

Sticky Fingers Pie

1 cup molasses
1 cup brown sugar
1½ cups flour
½ teaspoon baking soda
⅔ cup hot water
½ cup butter
pinch of salt

Heat the water in a small pot, then add baking soda and molasses. When mixed, pour into a greased pie tin. Combine the flour, sugar, butter and salt in a bowl until it crumbles into tiny pellets. Pour them on top of the molasses. Bake in a moderate oven for half an hour or until the crumbs are brown.

Rebel Crunch

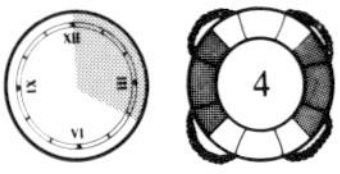

3 cups peanuts, shelled and crushed
3 cups sugar
1 pound grated semi-sweet chocolate
2 teaspoons butter

Heat the sugar in a frying pan until it melts into a syrup. Remove from the flame, add peanuts, chocolate and butter, then mix well. Pour on to a greased cookie (baking) sheet. Let cool, break into pieces and serve.

Peace-pipe Fudge

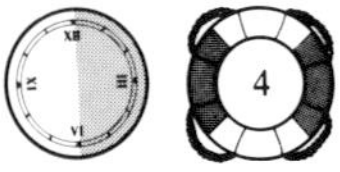

4 cups sugar
4 ounces unsweetened chocolate
2 teaspoons vanilla essence (extract)
Pinch of salt

Heat the chocolate and milk in a saucepan, stirring slowly until the mixture is blended. Add sugar and salt. After mixture boils and begins to thicken, remove from the stove and add butter and vanilla. Don't stir. Let cool till lukewarm, then beat again and pour at once into a buttered tin. Serve when firm. Variations:

1 Add chopped nuts and/or marshmallow cream.
2 To make the fudge richer, use cream instead of milk.
3 If you have no chocolate, use a cup of cocoa instead. In that case add only 3 cups of sugar instead of 4.

Dead Man's Soufflé

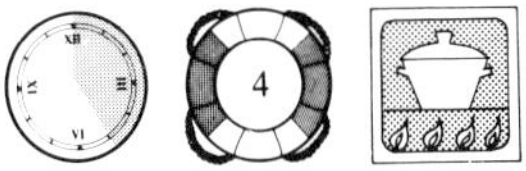

5 ounces bitter-sweet chocolate
4 fingers rum
3 tablespoons sugar
6 eggs, separated

Melt the chocolate and stir in the rum. Add the sugar, the beaten egg yolks, then fold in the stiff egg whites. Pour into a buttered casserole and bake in a hot oven for about 15 minutes.

Cannon Rum Balls

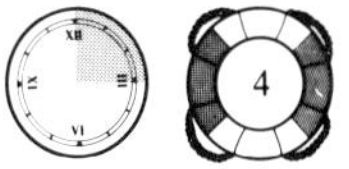

5 cups vanilla biscuits (cookies), crushed
1 cup nuts, chopped
1 cup icing sugar
½–1 cup dark rum
¼ cup corn syrup
2 tablespoons cocoa

Combine all ingredients in a bowl. Dust your hands with icing sugar, then mix well. Roll the dough into balls about an inch in diameter. Coat with sugar and store in a tightly closed container for several days before serving. Of course, the more rum, the better.

Coconut Bread

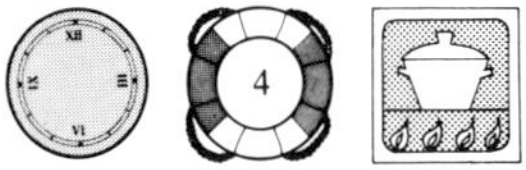

½ a coconut, grated
¾ pound flour
2 tablespoon baking powder
1 cup milk
⅓ stick (1½ oz) butter or margarine
pinch of cinnamon
pinch of salt
⅓ pound sugar

Combine flour, sugar, salt, cinnamon and baking powder. Slowly add the coconut, milk and butter and mix into a dough. Place in greased or floured baking dish and bake in a moderate oven for about an hour.

Grapeshot Pudding

3 fingers sherry
3 eggs
¾ cup sugar
½ teaspoon baking powder
2 tablespoons flour
1 cup raisins
handful of nuts, chopped
pinch of salt

Combine the eggs and sugar, then add baking powder, flour, nuts and raisins. Mix well. Pour into a greased baking dish and bake in a moderate oven for about half an hour. Just before serving, douse with sherry.

Gunner's Cake

6–8 slices of bread rusks
3 eggs, separated
juice of 1 lemon
juice of 1 orange
¼ pound sugar
¼ cup white wine
2 tablespoons icing sugar
pinch of cinnamon

Beat egg yolks, lemon juice, orange juice and all the sugar except one tablespoon in a bowl until foamy. Add the crumbled bread rusks, cinnamon and unbeaten egg whites. Mix well. Pour into a greased baking dish and bake in a moderate oven for about 1 hour. When ready, remove from the dish and pour on a sauce of hot white wine and 1 tablespoon sugar. Sprinkle with icing sugar.

Armistice Cake

2 cups sugar
1 cup butter
1 cup milk
3 cups flour
4 eggs
2 teaspoons baking powder
1 teaspoon vanilla essence (extract)
pinch of salt

Mix the sugar, flour, salt and baking powder. In a separate bowl cream the sugar and butter, then add it to the dry ingredients while gradually pouring in the milk. Mix in eggs and the vanilla. Pour into greased baking tins and bake in a moderate oven for about half an hour.

For the middle:

3 fingers rum
2 cups sugar
3–4 tablespoons butter

Mix the sugar and butter, then slowly add the rum. When the mixture is smooth and creamy, spread between the layers.

For the top:

1 cup sugar
1 egg white, beaten
1 tablespoon vanilla essence (extract)
½ cup water

Bring the sugar and water to the boil and stir until the mixture is stiff. Fold in the egg white, then the vanilla essence (extract). Beat until creamy.

Hangman's Grog

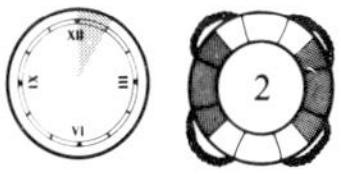

4 fingers rum
4 tablespoons sugar
2 glasses boiling water
juice of 1 lemon
pinch of cinnamon

Pour rum in a mug, add lemon, sugar, cinnamon and lastly the boiling water. Mix well, and serve.

Whaler's grog – Just before serving, add a pat of butter to each mug.

Tea grog – Use tea instead of boiling water, and add a slice of lemon.

Chapter 12

Five O'clock Tea

'There was always plenty of fresh bread as the "Kock" baked twice a week. At coffee-time on Saturdays he produced a special loaf with an elaborate design on top sprinkled with sugar and sometimes with fruit in it. The arrival of the special loaf marked the end of the working week and always put us in a good temper.'

Eric Newby, The Last Grain Race

Milky Way

The Cook of the schooner *Milky Way*
cordially invites you to tea on the afterdeck.
The esteemed chef
Jean-Claude Bidon, of the tramp steamer
Vagabond, will be present and
discuss his famous book,

The Nautical Cooking Almanac

U.R.W.G.

Mata Hari Tea

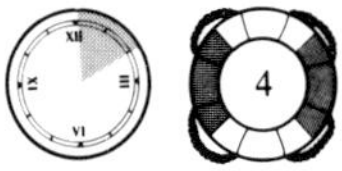

3 tea-bags
8 cloves
1 teaspoons cinnamon
1 cup orange juice
3 tablespoons honey

Heat the cloves and cinnamon in one cup of water, and let simmer for 5 minutes. Add honey, another cup of water, orange juice and bring to the boil. Drop in the tea-bags and let steep. Strain out the tea and spices and serve.

Zanzibar Spiced Tea

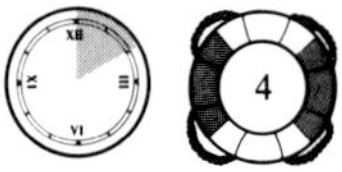

2 tablespoons black tea
2 cloves
juice of 1 lemon
juice of 1 orange
$\frac{1}{4}$ cup sugar
1 quart boiling water

Pour the water over the tea, add cloves, and let steep for several minutes. Strain, add fruit juices and sugar. Serve hot.

Mokka Java

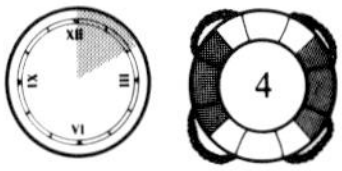

2 teaspoons instant coffee
2 tablespoons cocoa powder
2 tablespoons sugar
2 cups hot milk
1 teaspoon vanilla essence (extract)
pinch of salt

Mix instant coffee, cocoa powder, sugar and salt in a small pot. Add $\frac{1}{2}$ cup of water and bring to a boil. Pour in the hot milk, and another cup of water. Let boil for 1–2 minutes. Mix in vanilla essence (extract), and serve.

Café Martinique

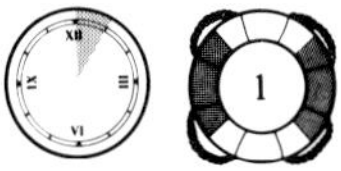

1 cup hot coffee
2 fingers rum
1–2 teaspoons sugar
1 clove
slice of orange peel
pinch of cinnamon

Put sugar in a small pot. Add the clove, orange peel and cinnamon. Pour in the coffee and rum and heat. Do not boil.

Paradise Island Coffee

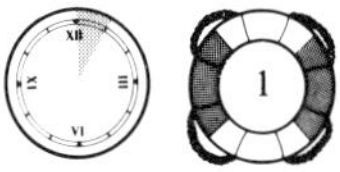

1 cup coconut milk
1 tablespoon sugar
1 cup strong coffee
1 tablespoon toasted coconut flakes
pinch of cinnamon

Heat the milk and mix in the sugar. Then add the coffee. Sprinkle on cinnamon and coconut flakes just before serving.

Café Française

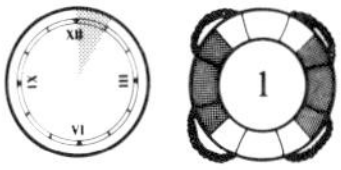

1 cup hot coffee
1–2 teaspoons sugar
2 fingers cognac

Add sugar to the hot coffee and mix well. Carefully pour the cognac on top of the coffee, light it and serve.

Peanut Butter Cakes

½ cup peanut butter
2 cups flour
3 teaspoons baking powder
3 tablespoons sugar
1 egg, beaten
1–1½ cups milk
2 tablespoons cooking oil
pinch of salt

Mix the dry ingredients – flour, baking powder, salt and sugar. Then work in the peanut butter, egg, cooking oil and enough milk to make a thick, lumpy batter. Mould into small cakes, place on a greased baking sheet, and bake in a hot oven for 20–30 minutes.

Spice Bread

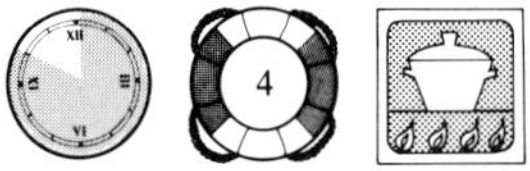

1 cup sugar
3 fingers rum
4 cups flour
2 teaspoons baking soda
2 teaspoons cinnamon
¾ cup honey
1½ cups hot water
2 teaspoons liquid aniseed flavouring
pinch of salt

Dissolve the honey in water, then mix thoroughly with rum and dry ingredients. Bake in a greased tin for 45 minutes to one hour. Cool before serving, and if possible, allow to cure overnight.

Banana Bread

3 ripe bananas
2 eggs, beaten
2 cups flour
½ cup sugar
1 teaspoon baking powder
2–3 tablespoons water
1 handful nuts, crushed
pinch of salt

Crush the bananas, and mix in the eggs, flour, baking powder and salt. Slowly fold in the sugar and crushed nuts. Place in a greased baking tin and bake for about an hour in a moderate oven.

Cheese Bread

2 cups grated cheese
5 cups flour
2 tablespoons butter or margarine
1 teaspoon salt
1 cup warm water
2 tablespoons sugar
1 packet (1 oz) of yeast
1 cup milk

Mix the milk, sugar, salt and butter in a casserole. Heat, scald and set to one side to cool. Dissolve the yeast in water, then add it to the milk mixture, along with 2 cups of flour. Mix well, and work into a dough, gradually stirring in the cheese and the rest of the flour. Knead, cover and set aside to rise in a warm place for an hour. Punch down, knead and let rise again. Bake in a moderate oven for about an hour. Cover the top of the baking pan to prevent the crust from burning.

Dublin Oatcakes

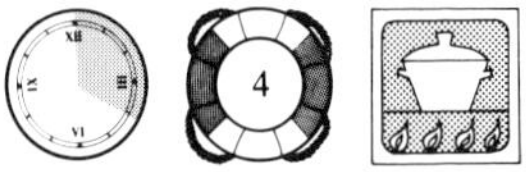

1 cup oatmeal
½ teaspoon baking powder
1 tablespoonbutter or margarine, melted
1 tablespoon salt
¼ cup hot water

Mix the dry ingredients, then fold in the butter. Add water, teaspoon by teaspoon, until the dough becomes a thick paste. Form into round patties. Bake on a greased sheet in a moderate oven for about 15 minutes.

Chapter 13

A Mermaid Climbs on Board

'On Friday morn as we set sail,
It was not far from land,
O, there I spied a fair pretty maid,
With a comb and a glass in her hand.'

The Mermaid, *anonymous*

'What a woman on board? We had never thought about this. But we had to take her. We couldn't simply throw her over the side. Besides, she was too nice for that. But I'd like to make it clear we wouldn't have thrown an old witch over the side either.'

Graf Felix Luckner, Seeteufel's World Cruise

What woman can resist an invitation for dinner on board your yacht, a candlelight evening filled with exotic dishes and lore of the sea.

But the setting must be right: at anchor in a secluded bay, the boat clean, but deliberately not spotless, and the dinner pre-cooked so that you can put it together with absent-minded ease.

Your logbook lies open on the table so she can glance at a few of your recipes, collected, of course, from old fishermen in the Azores, tribesmen in New Guinea or the chef of the royal yacht.

Your only *faux pas* is the knot with which you tied the dinghy's painter. Somehow, it has come loose and the dinghy has drifted to shore.

Menu I

White Slaver's Soup

1½ cups white wine
1 egg yolk
4 tablespoons sugar
1 tablespoon cornflour (cornstarch)
pinch of cinnamon
dash of lemon juice

Boil 1½ cups of water, then add cinnamon, lemon juice and cornflour (cornstarch). Mix well and remove from heat. Add wine, sugar and egg yolk. Mix again and serve.

Red Wine Chicken

1 chicken, cut into pieces
2 cups red wine
6 tablespoons butter
¼ pound bacon, diced
4 onions, sliced
1 carrot, sliced
3 sticks of celery, sliced
2 potatoes, sliced
2 cups of bouillon
2 cloves garlic, crushed
1 bay leaf
pinch of thyme
salt and pepper

In a large casserole, fry the onions in butter until brown. Then add potatoes, celery, carrots, garlic, and finally the chicken pieces and diced bacon. Pour in the bouillon and wine, salt, pepper and spices and let simmer for several hours. Add a cup of cognac, if you can spare it.

Rum and Bananas

4 bananas, peeled and cut into strips
1 cup rum
2 tablespoons butter

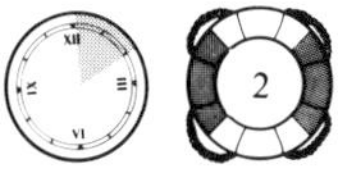

2 tablespoons sugar
½ teaspoon cinnamon
dash of lemon juice

Melt the butter in a deep frying pan. Add bananas and cover with sugar, cinnamon and lemon juice. Fry on both sides until brown. Turn down the flame, add rum, light with a match and serve immediately.

Menu II

Gin and Crabmeat Soup

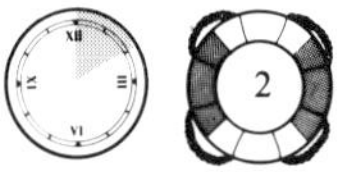

1 medium can crabmeat
2 fingers gin
1 tablespoon butter
1 cup water
palmful of parsley
salt and pepper

Mix water and crabmeat, heat and stir until the meat has broken into fine pieces. Add salt, pepper and butter. Remove from the stove, and just before serving mix in the gin and sprinkle on the parsley.

White Wine and Clams

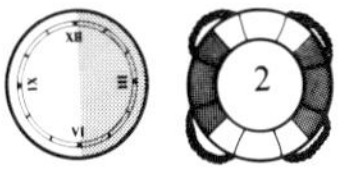

4 pounds clams
1 bottle white wine
¼ stick (1 oz) butter or margarine
2 tablespoons flour
4 onions, chopped
1 tablespoon tomato juice
palmful of parsley
pinch of pepper

Place the cleaned clams in a large pot. Add the wine and cook until the clams open. Transfer the clams to a large serving bowl, leaving the juice in the pot. In a frying pan heat the butter and flour, then add half the clam juice and the onions. Let mixture come to a boil, then add the rest of the clam juice and the tomato juice. Mix and pour the sauce over the clams. Sprinkle on the parsley and serve.

Port and Onions

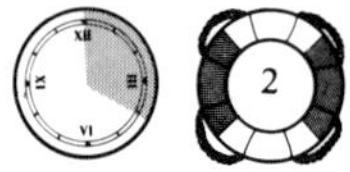

8 small onions, peeled
1 glass port wine
2 tablespoons olive oil
½ glass vinegar
2 tablespoons sugar
salt and pepper

Put olive oil and onions in a skillet and cook until they begin to soften. Then add wine, vinegar, sugar, salt and pepper. Continue cooking until the onions are brown and the syrup thick.

Cointreau Soufflé

3 egg whites
2 fingers cointreau
3 tablespoons sugar
3 tablespoons orange marmalade

Beat the egg whites until stiff, while slowly adding sugar. Mix in marmalade, then pour into a greased baking tin and bake in a moderate oven for half an hour. Just before serving, add the cointreau.

Menu III

Cognac and Oxtail Soup

1 medium can oxtail soup
2 fingers cognac
½ large can sliced pineapple
2 tablespoons coconut flakes
2 tablespoons pineapple syrup

Heat the soup and add the pineapple, pineapple syrup and cognac. Sprinkle on the coconut flakes and place in a hot oven until the crust is brown.

Applejack Omelette

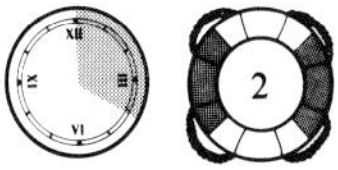

6 eggs
2 fingers applejack (calvados) – or rum
2 apples – peeled, cored and sliced
½ stick (2 oz) butter or margarine
2 teaspoons flour
2 tablespoons brown sugar
½ cup milk
salt and pepper

Melt butter in a frying pan. Add apples and applejack. Mix flour, eggs, milk, salt and pepper in a bowl and beat well. Then pour into the frying pan. After turning the omelette, sprinkle on the brown sugar.

Rum Carrots

1 pound carrots – scraped and sliced
3 fingers rum
1 cup butter
1 teaspoon sugar
1 teaspoon salt

Melt the butter in a casserole. Add the carrots, salt, sugar and rum. Cover and bake in a moderate oven for 45 minutes.

Brandied Peaches

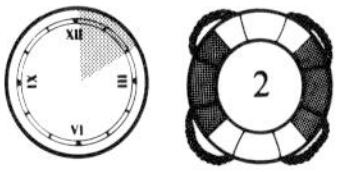

1 medium can peaches
3 fingers cognac
2 tablespoons sugar

Place peaches – minus the syrup – in a bowl, and marinate in cognac and sugar for half an hour before serving.

Chapter 14

The Dogwatch

'The only time when we could be said to take any pleasure was at night and morning, when we were allowed a tin pot full of hot tea (or, as the sailors significantly call it, "water bewitched") sweetened with molasses. This, bad as it was, was still warm and comforting, and, together with our sea biscuits and cold salt beef, made a meal.'

Richard Henry Dana, Two Years Before the Mast

The sea is calm and the boat steers herself. The gentle snores of the crew drift out of the hatch. You sit alone in the cockpit, leaning against the mizzen mast and stare up at the constellations. It's a time to think or dream.

Beside you is a cup of spicy grog well laced with rum. You sip it slowly and nibble a sandwich.

The clock strikes four bells, but it's a shame to leave such a beautiful night and go below. You shake the thermos and find it's still half full. Perhaps you'll stand the next watch as well.

The Russian Helmsman

3 fingers vodka
2 tablespoons sugar
1 egg yolk

Mix the egg yolk and sugar until a cream, then add the vodka.

Normandy Grog

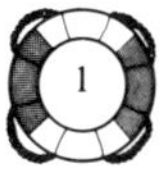

2 fingers calvados or applejack
1 cup hot apple cider
1 tablespoon honey
pinch of cinnamon

Dogwatch Grog

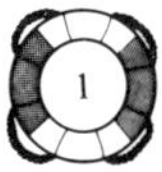

2 fingers rum
1 egg, beaten
1 tablespoon sugar
$\frac{3}{4}$ cup boiling water

First combine the sugar and the egg, mix well, then add the rum and water.

The Taffrail Comrade

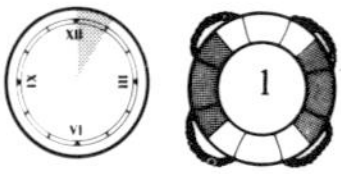

1 cup hot beef bouillon
2 fingers vodka
dash of Worcester sauce
dash of lemon juice

Mix in a mug, adding the vodka last.

Bilge Bouillon

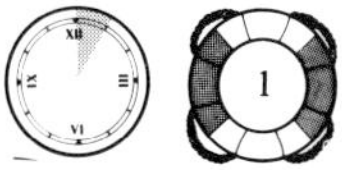

1 cup hot beef bouillon
3 fingers white wine
palmful of grated cheese

Hot Milk Grog

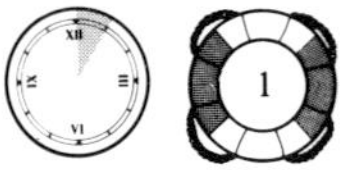

2 fingers rum
$\frac{3}{4}$ cup hot milk
1–2 tablespoons sugar
pinch of nutmeg

Pour rum in a mug, add sugar and hot milk, then sprinkle on the nutmeg.

Windward Tea

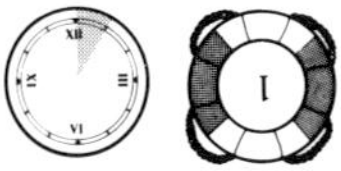

3 fingers rum
1 cup strong tea
1 pineapple ring
1 tablespoon sugar

Soak the pineapple in rum for a few minutes, then add the hot tea and sugar.

Neptune's Coffee

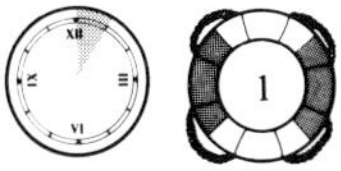

1 cup strong coffee
2 egg yolks
2 tablespoons sugar

Mix egg yolks and sugar. Beat well, add coffee and heat until it steams. Do not boil.

Brooklyn Sandwich

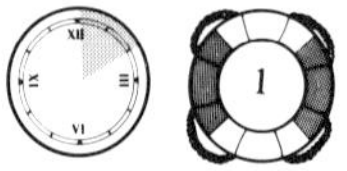

2 slices toast
1 egg
1 small onion, sliced
1 tablespoon tomato sauce
salt and pepper

Fry the egg in butter, then place it on a slice of toast. Season and add tomato sauce and onion. Cover with toast and serve hot.

A Hot-Beer Sandwich

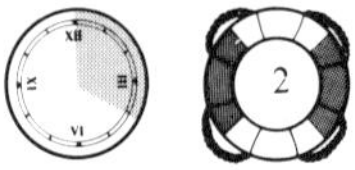

½ pound minced (hamburger) beef
½ onion, chopped
¼ green pepper, chopped
1 small can beer
½ cup cheese, grated
2 tablespoons butter or margarine
dash of Tabasco sauce

Place butter in a frying pan and cook onion, pepper and meat until brown. Add beer and Tabasco sauce, then gradually stir in the cheese until it has melted. Serve over muffins, biscuits (creamcrackers) or toast.

Chapter 15

Trade Winds Cooking

'Many excellent cooks are spoiled by going into the arts.'

Paul Gauguin

'What did best on the raft, along with the crabs, were barnacles from an inch to an inch and a half long. They grew in hundreds, especially on the lee side of the raft, and as fast as we put the old ones into the soup kettle new larvae took root and grew up. The barnacles tasted fresh and delicate; we picked the seaweed as salad, and it was eatable, though not so good.'

Thor Heyerdahl, Kon-Tiki Expedition

'Taking things by and large, as sailors say, I got on fairly well in the matter of provisions even on the long voyage across the Pacific. I always found some small stores to help the fare of luxuries; what I lacked of fresh meat was made up in fresh fish, at least while in the trade-winds, where flying fish crossing on the wing at night would hit the sails and fall on the deck, sometimes two or three of them, sometimes a dozen. Every morning except when the moon was large I got a bountiful supply by merely picking them up from the lee scuppers. All tinned meats went begging.'

Joshua Slocum, Sailing Alone Around the World

Position: 6° 10′ S—95° 23 ′ W
Weather: Wind – Force 4, Sky – clear
Sea: Gentle, with long, graceful swells
Sail Plan: jib, staysail, main, topsail and mizzen

'Our 42nd day from Valparaiso. I spent the morning repairing the storm sail, the one that saved us off the Horn. Then I climbed out on the bowsprit and watched the dolphins surf in the bow wave. Never have I been so at ease with the world. Then, suddenly, I felt as though I was back in Paris, standing in front of a restaurant on the Rue Mouftarde and smelling the herbs and garlic simmer in butter.

'But it wasn't a dream. Mac was in the galley preparing my favourite Trade Winds meal.'

Polynesian Soup

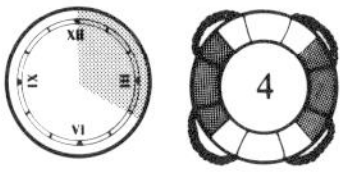

$\frac{1}{4}$ pound coconut, grated
1 quart bouillon
$\frac{1}{4}$ pound flour
$\frac{1}{2}$ small can condensed milk
pinch of nutmeg
salt and cayenne pepper

Heat the bouillon and coconut in a large pot, cook for about 10 minutes, then add nutmeg, salt and pepper. Mix in the flour and let boil for 5 minutes. Stir constantly. Add the milk just before serving.

Onion Soup

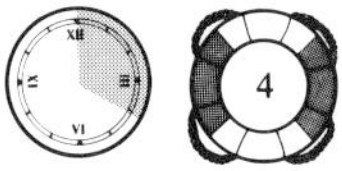

6 large onions, sliced
4 cups beef bouillon
$\frac{1}{2}$ cup grated Parmesan cheese
2 tablespoons olive oil
2 cloves garlic, crushed
$\frac{1}{2}$ cup white wine
6–8 slices of toast
pinch of salt

In a large saucepan, fry the onions in butter until they are soft. Heat the bouillon in another pot, then pour it over the onions. Simmer for about 10 minutes. Make a paste of the garlic and olive oil then rub it on the toast. Float it on top of the soup, then sprinkle on the cheese. Cover, and serve as soon as the cheese has melted.

Chinese Egg Drop Soup

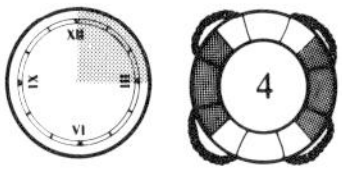

1 egg, beaten
2 medium cans chicken soup
1 onion, minced
2 tablespoons cornflour (cornstarch)
salt and pepper

Heat the chicken soup, then slowly add the cornflour (cornstarch). Pour in the egg, which should separate into shreds. Add the onion, salt and pepper to taste, and serve.

Raw Fish à la Tahitienne

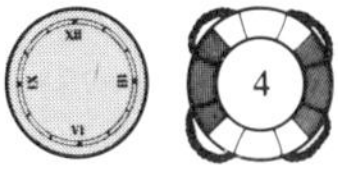

4 fillets fresh tuna
6 limes
1 cup coconut milk
2 tomatoes, chopped
1 onion, chopped
1 carrot, grated
pinch of salt

Cut the fish into bite-sized pieces, place in a pan and squeeze the limes over them. Add salt and let stand for at least one hour or preferably longer. Remove some of the juice and mix with the other vegetables and coconut milk. Pour the sauce over the fish and serve.

Gloucester Fish Omelette

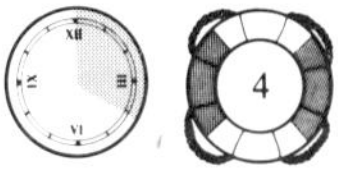

2 fresh fish fillets, cut into chunks
6 eggs
1 onion, diced
1 green pepper, chopped
1 can tomato juice
2 tablespoons butter or margarine
pinch of rosemary
salt and pepper

Fry the fish in butter until almost cooked – about 5 minutes. Then beat the eggs and pour into the pan. When the eggs begin to firm, add onion, green pepper, spices and can of tomato juice. Mix gently. Cook until the sauce begins to boil, then serve.

Equator Eggs

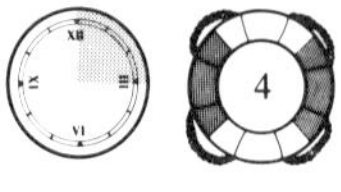

4 eggs
4 ripe bananas, peeled
4 slices of ham
2 tablespoons butter or margarine
pinch of paprika
salt and pepper

Cut the bananas in half and fry them in one tablespoon of butter. Then place them in the bottom of a hot casserole and cover them with ham. Using the other tablespoon of butter, fry the eggs, then place on top of the ham. Serve with toast and butter.

Turtle in a Milky Sea

4 cooked fillets of turtle
6 hard-boiled eggs
2 cups cream
2 tablespoons butter or margarine
pinch of powdered cloves
salt and pepper

Separate egg whites and yolks, then mix yolks and butter into a paste. Heat the cream and fold in the egg yolk paste. Cut the turtle into small chunks and add them. Season and cook for 10–15 minutes. Serve with diced egg whites.

Shark Steaks

4 steaks cut from near the shark's tail
1 egg
handful of breadcrumbs
3 tablespoons butter or margarine
juice of one lemon
1 green pepper, sliced
4 tablespoons cooking oil
pinch of sage

Beat the egg and lemon juice together, then place in a pan. Add the steaks, cover with a sprinkling of sage, and let stand for one hour. Turn and let the steaks marinate for another hour. Heat the butter and oil in a frying pan. Coat the steaks with breadcrumbs, then cook for 10–12 minues, turning only once. Serve with strips of raw green pepper.

Fish and Rice Casserole

1 pound fresh fish fillets, chopped in pieces
¼ pound rice
6 tablespoons cooking oil
1 small can condensed milk
2 eggs
4 tomatoes, sliced
2 palmfuls parsley
1 teaspoon garlic powder
pinch of salt

In a casserole, fry the rice in half the cooking oil until the grains become glazed. Add 3 cups of hot water and cook for 15 minutes. Mix garlic, salt and rest of oil into a sauce and marinate the fish. Grease a baking dish and pour in half the rice. Add a layer of tomato slices, then a layer of fish – another layer of tomatoes, one of fish, and finally the rest of the rice. Mix milk, parsley and eggs in a bowl, then pour over the mixture. Bake in a moderate oven for about half an hour.

Flying Fish Pizza

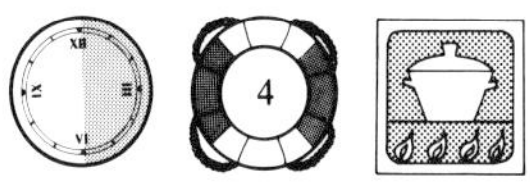

4–6 medium-sized flying fish
¼ pound flour
1 packet (1 oz) yeast
1 can tomato purée
3 tablespoons olive oil
½ teaspoon oregano
3–4 ounces cheese
pinch of salt

Mix the yeast with a little warm water and set to one side. Add about ¼ cup of water to the flour and work into a dough. Mix in the yeast and salt. Knead well, roll into a ball, cover and put in a warm place for an hour. Then roll the dough into a disc. Mix the tomato purée and oil and spread it on. Add the cheese and flying fish. Garnish with oregano and bake in a hot oven for about 20 minutes. If no flying fish have landed on your deck, use strips of tuna or dorado.

Creole Potatoes

2 pounds potatoes, peeled and sliced
3 onions, chopped
3 tomatoes, sliced
3 green peppers, sliced
2 tablespoons cooking oil
1 teaspoon black pepper
pinch of salt.

Boil the potatoes, drain them and place them in a warm bowl. Grease a baking tin, and in alternating layers add potatoes, onions, tomatoes and green peppers. Sprinkle a little salt and pepper on each layer. Pour oil over the top and bake in a moderate oven for 20 minutes.

Glazed Onions

6–8 small onions, peeled
4 tablespoons sugar
2 tablespoons butter or margarine

Sauté the whole onions in butter until they are brown. Then sprinkle on sugar. Add enough water to cover them, and simmer until it has evaporated and the sugar has turned to caramel.

Mangoes in Wine

8 ripe mangoes
1 bottle red wine
2 tablespoons sugar
dash of vanilla essence (extract)

Peel the mangoes, cut them in small pieces, and place them in a baking dish. Pour in the wine, vanilla essence (extract) and sugar. Bake for half an hour in a moderate oven. Serve when cooled.

Pineapplekraut

1 can sauerkraut
1 small can chopped pineapple
1 cup white wine
¼ stick (1 oz) butter or margarine
1 tablespoon vinegar
pinch of white pepper

Place sauerkraut and wine in a casserole and let simmer slowly. Gradually add the butter, then the vinegar and pepper. Fold in the pineapple and mix well. If the taste is too sour, add some juice from the pineapple.

Chocolate Coconut Poi

1 cup shredded coconut
3 cups oatmeal
2 cups sugar
½ cup butter or margarine
½ cup milk
5 tablespoons cocoa powder

Heat the milk, butter and sugar in a pan. As soon as it comes to the boil, remove from the stove. Add the rest of the ingredients, mix well and let cool for about 10 minutes. Poi can be eaten in a bowl – traditionally with fingers – or dough can be dropped on a sheet and baked like cookies, or in a tin as a cake.

Flying Fish

A breakfast of flying fish is a delicacy only sailors know. Marinated in lemon juice, garlic and finely chopped onions, it becomes one of the most succulent creatures inhabiting the sea.

Strangely enough, flying fish don't fly. They glide, sometimes as far as a quarter of a mile. When chased by a predator, they break the surface, spread their wing-like fins and with a final sculling motion of their tails, skim over the waves. About a hundred species exist and populate every warm ocean.

The easiest way to catch them is to sit in the cockpit at night, flashlight in hand, and wait for one to fly into your lap.

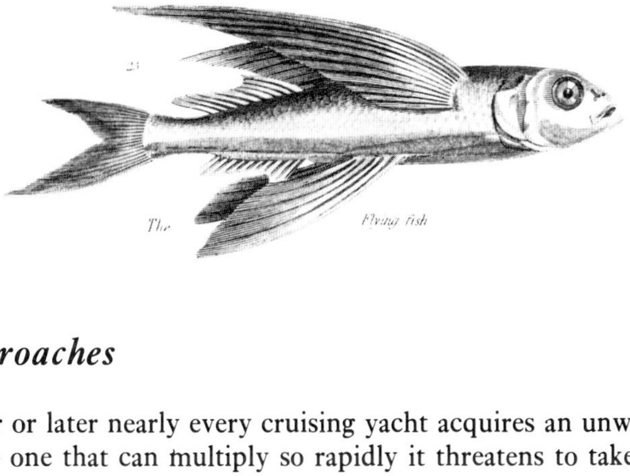

Cockroaches

Sooner or later nearly every cruising yacht acquires an unwanted crew – one that can multiply so rapidly it threatens to take over the boat.

Dealing with these persistent and apparently intelligent creatures can be an annoying problem. Virtually all the powders, sprays and poisoned foods work to some degree, but careful experimentation may be necessary as cockroaches can develop resistant strains. Often something as simple as a mixture of equal amounts of sugar and borax placed in a dish will kill them off.

However, victory can be deceiving. The eggs left behind may take as long as several months to hatch, and then, nearly overnight, the boat is infested again.

Preserving Meat

Two traditional methods:

1 Cut the meat – beef, lamb or pork – into strips or cubes and fry until well cooked. Drain off the fat, let cool, then place in a box or plastic container. Cover completely with lard and seal air-tight. If some of the meat is removed, be sure the rest is well covered with lard before re-sealing the container.

2 Cut the meat into thin slices, cover with rock salt, and lay in the sun. Turn and re-salt several times. When it becomes dry, hang on a line between the shrouds until hard. Store in a dry place and at least every two weeks hang it in the sun again for a few hours. To use: soak for a day in fresh water, changing the water 2–3 times.

Storing Cabbages

Cabbages will normally keep for about two weeks, but if stored with care they will remain fresh for four weeks or longer. Place them in nets slung between the beams, make a hole in each stalk with an ice pick or screw driver, and fill the holes with a little fresh water every two or three days.

Storing Lemons

If stored properly, lemons will remain fresh for months. Perhaps the easiest way is to wrap them in paper or aluminium foil and pack them in baskets or crates. But avoid having too many layers as pressure will hasten spoilage. Another method is to thread them on a line, passing the needle through the nipples, and hang them in the forepeak between the deck beams. Tie a knot after each lemon so that they can't slide together.

Eggs for the Voyage

Fresh eggs, stored in a dry, cool place in the bottom of the boat, will keep for about 2 weeks. For longer periods up to three months, the shells must be made air-tight.

1 Coat them with Vaseline.

2 Soak them in a solution of 8 parts water and 1 part slaked lime.

3 Place them in a wooden box and cover completely with fine salt.

Or probably the simplest and best method

4 Paint the eggs with varnish.

Turn the cartons over once a week.

Three Ways to Make Coconut Milk

Grate the meat of one coconut as finely as possible. Next:

1 Soak it in the water of the coconut for half an hour, then strain through a handkerchief or a piece of cheesecloth.

2 Pour boiling water over the meat – not the water from the coconut – and let it soak for one hour. Strain through the cheesecloth.

3 For a richer flavour, perfect for curries, use hot milk instead of water.

When dried, the grated meat makes an excellent topping for cookies, soufflés and cakes.

A refreshing Polynesian drink can be made from the milk of five coconuts – prepared with coconut water – mixed with one quart of sea water.

'Interview' with the Cook of the Spray

Interviewer: Could you please tell us, in your own words, what is the real story of the *Spray*'s circumnavigation?

Cook: Well, first of all, let me clear up one myth. Old man Slocum wasn't alone. I was below decks the whole time cooking. The trip was my fault, I suppose. Joshua never really wanted to sail around the world. But after I told him about the fantastic steaks we'd get in Argentina, the roast pig in Polynesia and the grilled lamb in Australia, he just had to go. We went from one place to another, eating and drinking our fill, till one day we wound up back in Boston once again. And by the way, putting those tacks on the deck down in Tierra del Fuego to keep the natives off – that was my idea.

'Interview' with the Cook of the Bounty

Interviewer: Could you please tell us, in your own words, what really happened on board the *Bounty*?

Cook: Well, I suppose it was my fault. You see, I wanted to make a nice onion soup for the crew so I stole a couple of gallons of fresh water. While it was heating on the stove, old man Blyth stuck his head in the galley. As you know, he ran a tight ship. He was just about to keel-haul me when my friend Fletcher Christian rallied the crew and saved my life. We had no other choice but to put Blyth and most of the officers in a boat. Of course, I gave them enough food and water to get them to Timor.

Chapter 16

What shall we do to get the Sailor Drunk?

'. . . I lived on rum, I tell you. It's been meat and drink, and man and wife,to me; and if I'm not to have my rum now I'm a poor old hulk on a lee shore.'

Long John Silver in Treasure Island, *Robert Louis Stevenson*

'Our crew fell in with some who belonged to the other vessels, and, sailor-like, steered for the first grog-shop. . . . It is the universal custom with sailors for each one, in his turn, to treat the whole, calling for a glass all round, and obliging every one who is present, even to the keeper of the shop, to take a glass with him . . . for drink you must, every time; and if you drink with one, and not with another, it is always taken as an insult.'

Richard Henry Dana, Two Years Before the Mast

The love affair between sailors and alcohol is passionate, legendary and still very real today. When the crew is ready to lighten their spirits, an event which occurs frequently on a good boat, the Cook mixes a tasty punch – plentiful enough to fill everyone's mug many times over, and potent enough to break even the meanest bosun. Of course, the boat is securely anchored, sea shanties are playing on the tape recorder, and yarns of previous voyages are spliced between the drinks.

Finally, singing raucously, the crew departs for the port in search of adventure. As they stumble down the dock, swaying back and forth as though it were a pitching deck in a storm, the Cook looks on contentedly. He has done his job well.

Cook's Punch

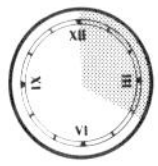

1 bottle rum or cognac
10 eggs
½ pound sugar
grated skin of two lemons
2 bottles soda water

Mix all ingredients in a large casserole. Heat on a low flame, and at the same time beat with an egg beater. When foam begins to rise, remove from stove and serve immediately.

Captain's Punch

2 bottles white wine
½ bottle rum
2 pounds sugar
juice of two lemons
3 cups water

Heat the water and stir in the sugar until it is dissolved. Then add wine and rum. Remove from the stove and flambé. Add the lemon juice and serve, hot or cold.

Wild Bunch Punch

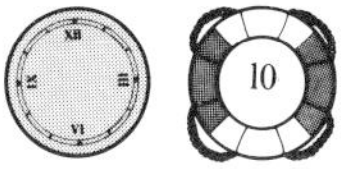

1 bottle dark rum
1 bottle sherry
1 quart green tea
½ bottle whisky
juice of 2 oranges
juice of 1 lemon

Mix everything. Then let stand for several hours before serving.

Forecastle Punch

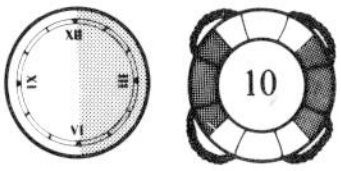

1 bottle brandy
1 bottle white wine
½ bottle dark rum
4 tablespoons sugar
juice of 10 lemons

Mix thoroughly and let stand for half an hour. Serve cold.

Admiral's Punch

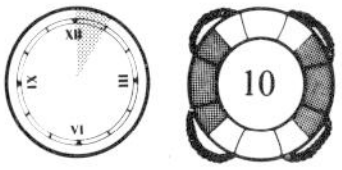

1 bottle champagne
1 glass brandy
1 glass curaçao
1 tablespoon sugar
2 bottles soda water

If possible, serve cold with crushed ice.

Fish-house Punch

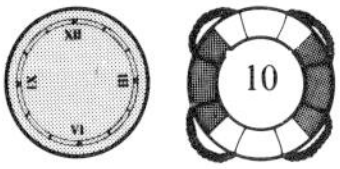

1 bottle light rum
½ bottle brandy
4 fingers peach brandy
juice of 2 lemons
1 cup water : ¼ cup sugar

Mix the water, lemon juice and sugar. Then add rum, brandy and peach brandy, and let stand for several hours. Serve cold.

Murmansk Coffee Punch

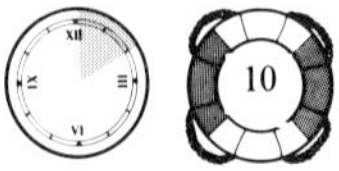

1 bottle red wine
$\frac{1}{2}$ bottle vodka
$\frac{1}{2}$–$\frac{3}{4}$ quart strong coffee
1 cup sugar

Mix wine, vodka and coffee. Heat and gradually add sugar. Serve hot.

The Piano Player's Egg Nog

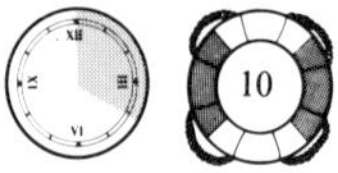

6 eggs
$\frac{1}{2}$ quart whisky
$\frac{1}{2}$ quart cream
$\frac{1}{2}$ bottle rum
1 quart milk
$\frac{1}{3}$ pound sugar

Separate egg whites and yolks. Beat the yolks, adding sugar gradually, then slowly pour in the rum, milk and cream. Add the whisky, and finally fold in the stiffly beaten egg whites. Chill, if possible, and serve.

Variation: Reduce the amount of whisky and add brandy.

Coffee Punch

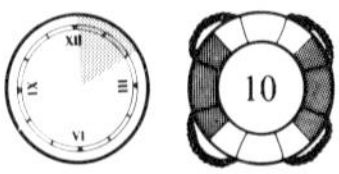

1 quart extra strong coffee
1 bottle port wine
1 bottle rum
$\frac{1}{2}$ pound brown sugar

Put the coffee, wine and rum in a pot and heat, but *do not boil.* Add sugar gradually and mix well. Serve hot.

Virgin Islands punch

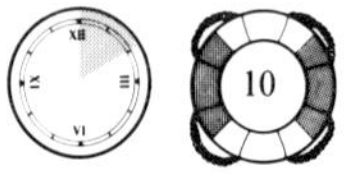

2 bottles rum
1 bottle cognac or brandy
1 cup peach or apricot liqueur
1 bottle lemon juice
1 quart of tea
1$\frac{1}{2}$ cups sugar

Chapter 17

What shall we do with the Drunken Sailor?

'I had seen whiskey drunk, such as whiskey and soda by the men of the clubs, but never as these men drank it, from pannikins and mugs, and from the bottles – great brimming drinks, each one of which was in itself a debauch.

But they did not stop at one or two. They drank and drank, and ever the bottles slipped forward and they drank more . . . In loud voices they shouted over the day's fighting, wrangled about details, or waxed affectionate and made friends with the men whom they had fought . . . It was a saturnalia.'

Jack London, Sea Wolf

'The wicked all are water-drinkers:
'Tis by the deluge clearly proved.'
Comte de Ségur

Drunkenness – *'Deaths of seamen are recorded every year either as a direct result of the excessive drinking of liquor, or from accidents, such as falling from wharves and gangways, whilst under the influence of drink. In addition, there have been cases where men, brought on board in a semi-comatose condition, have been simply put to bed to sleep it off and have been found dead some hours later either as a result of absorbing a fatal quantity of alcohol from their stomachs or by being "choked", i.e., asphyxiated, by their own vomit. Being "drunk" is therefore, at worst, a step towards death, and it is a condition which, common though it may be, should never be ignored or regarded as merely funny. On the contrary, men returning on board in a severely drunken state should be treated as sick persons requiring close watching and careful nursing if their lives are not to be further jeopardised.'*

The Ship Captain's Medical Guide, *Department of Trade and Industry*

Sailors Fight for their Cook

Twelve sailors, inebriated with cane juice, were involved in a violent argument in the Captain Cook bar last night. The dispute began when one ship's crew accused another of plotting to Shanghai their Cook. A fight broke out, and the Police were called. Reinforcements were necessary before order could be restored.

'Both crews were taken to the local jail to sober up. This morning, after paying 625 dollars in damages to the owner of the bar, they were released into the custody of the Cooks of their vessels.'

From: *The South Port Harbour News*

Sunrise Egg Nog

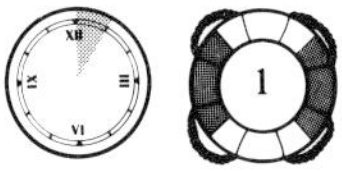

2 fingers brandy
1 finger curaçao
3 fingers milk
1 egg
1 tablespoon sugar

The Dawn comes up Like Thunder

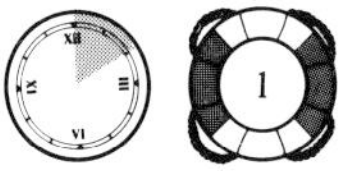

3 fingers scotch
1 tablespoon Pernod
juice of 1 lemon
white of 1 egg
2 tablespoons sugar

The Helping Hand

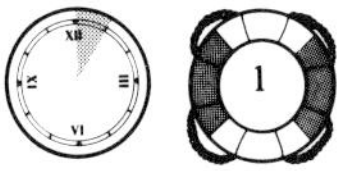

1 finger vodka
1 glass tomato juice
1 container yoghurt
1 garlic clove, crushed
dash of Worcestershire sauce
dash of Tabasco sauce
salt and pepper

Bloody Mary

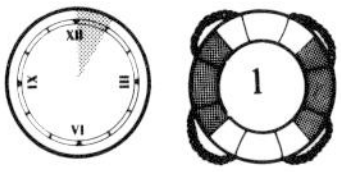

1 glass tomato juice
2 finger vodka
1 tablespoon lemon juice
dash of Worcestershire sauce
salt and pepper

Nelson's Coffee

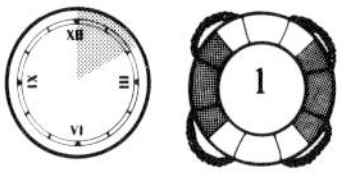

1 cup hot, strong coffee
2 fingers brandy
2 tablespoons sugar
twist of orange peel
dash of lemon juice

Liquid Breakfast

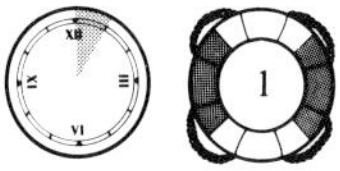

1 glass milk
1 banana, mashed
1 egg
1 teaspoon sugar
dash of lemon juice
ice, if possible

Huevos Rancheros

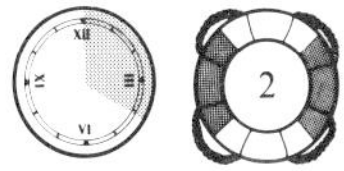

6 eggs
1 onion, chopped
1 can tomato juice
1 green pepper, chopped
3 tablespoons butter or margarine
1 small can mushrooms
½ teaspoon chilli powder
salt and pepper

Sauté the onion in butter, then mix in tomato sauce, green pepper and chilli powder. Add the eggs, sunny side up, the mushrooms and seasoning. Cover the pan and cook until eggs are firm.

Garlic Soup

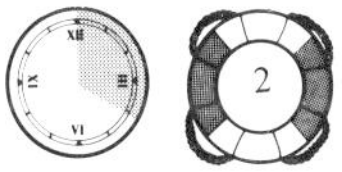

2 tablespoons garlic, crushed
⅓ cup olive oil
2 cups breadcrumbs
1 teaspoon paprika
4 cups water
¼ teaspoon cayenne pepper
2 eggs, beaten
palmful of chopped parsley
salt

Heat the olive oil in a casserole, then add garlic and cook until soft. Add breadcrumbs, paprika, water, cayenne pepper and let boil. Then simmer for 10 minutes without a cover. Stir in eggs, simmer a few moments more, then sprinkle on parsley and serve.

Red Cross

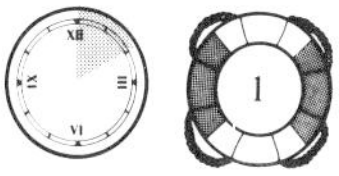

1 glass tomato juice
2 fingers gin
1 egg yolk
pinch of black pepper
pinch of celery salt

The Dutch Cure

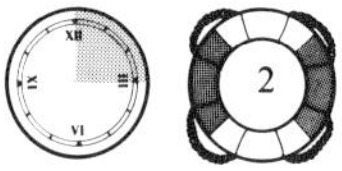

2 marinated herrings cut in small pieces
2 onions, sliced
1 pickle, chopped
1 apple, chopped
2 tablespoons cooking oil
1 tablespoon vinegar
½ cup milk
1 tablespoon mayonnaise
pinch of salt and pepper
pinch of dill

Combine apples, onions, herring and pickle. Make a sauce from the oil, vinegar, milk, mayonnaise, and salt and pepper. Mix well and pour over the herring mixture *the night before*, if possible. Serve on toast and sprinkle on dill.

Vitamins

Vitamins are a rather strange commodity. They're not elements in a chemical sense, nor foods as such, but, rather, organic compounds absolutely essential to the functioning of the human body.

The four major vitamins are:

1 Vitamin A

A deficiency results in: night blindness, dry, flaky skin, brittle, falling hair and a susceptibility to infectious diseases.

Common sources are: green vegetables, particularly water cress and parsley, cod liver oil and rich milk.

2 B Complex

A deficiency results in: nervousness, fatigue, headaches, rough skin, insomnia, gas and constipation.

Common sources are: whole grain foods, milk, yoghurt, liver, leafy green vegetables, and brewer's yeast.

3 Vitamin C

A deficiency results in: general fatigue and mild depression, headaches and aching limbs which eventually become scurvy (see page 80).

Common sources are: nearly every fresh vegetable and fruit, but especially citrus fruits.

4 Vitamin D

A deficiency results in: poor absorption of calcium and phosphorus, which are essential for strong bones and teeth.

Common sources are: milk, butter, eggs, fish oils and fresh green vegetables.

Chapter 18

Liferaft Cuisine

'The longest recorded survival by anyone is that of Second Steward Poon Lim in a ship's lifeboat in the Atlantic for 133 days. The boat had carried supplies and water which he was able to consume. His ship, the SS Ben Lomond, *had been torpedoed in the Atlantic 750 miles off the Azores on 23 November 1942. He was picked up on 5 April 1943 and was later awarded the BEM.'*

Guinness Book of Records

As the boat settles heavily in the water, and everyone jumps overboard, the Captain tries to save his logbook, the crew their hip flasks and credit cards.

And the Cook?

Hopefully, he has prepared for this moment, checked the liferaft before the voyage, and stowed it on deck where it is easily accessible.

The Captain may have lost the ship, but the Cook is still in command.

When he leaves the sinking galley, the most essential item he takes with him is an adequate water supply. The human body can exist for a surprisingly long time without food, but only a short period without water. Exactly how long that is depends on several factors – weather and body constitution, for example – but the upper limit appears to be about 10 or 11 days. Men have lived that long, and survived, without a drop of water.

Yet most liferafts found on yachts contain little or no fresh water. Manufacturers have tried to keep liferaft packs as small as possible to save deck space, and a proper water supply would increase their bulk enormously. Hence, an emergency water supply conveniently accessible on deck is nearly as important as the liferaft itself.

One way we've found to store liferaft water is to have three or four plastic jerrycans lashed on deck somewhere near the liferaft, either to the coachroof or the bulwarks. The cans should be only three-quarters full so that they will float, and should be covered with canvas to prevent the sun from hardening the plastic or stimulating the growth of algae in the water. They should be tied together with strong line, leaving at least a metre of slack between each can and several metres at the end which can be fastened to the raft. In this manner, they can be thrown overboard, if necessary, one by one.

No matter how much water the Cook takes with him into the liferaft, he still must be ready to replenish his supply with rainwater. Most liferafts with a canopy have a rain-catching device built into them; however, after a short time the rubberized fabric becomes encrusted with salt and must be washed clean before rain can be collected. Therefore, it is wise to prepare a plastic sheet with a tube coming from its centre. This can be placed in a

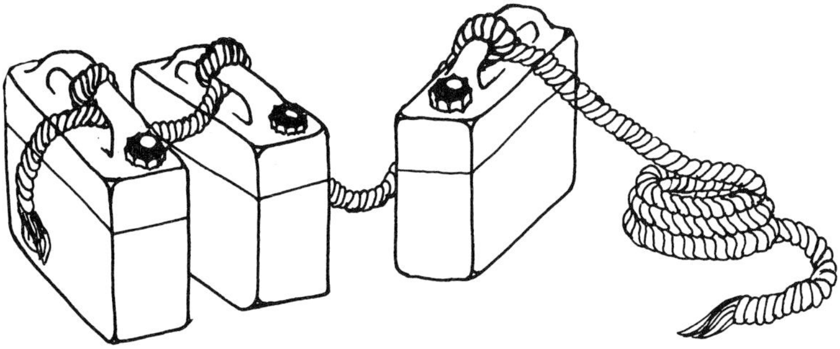

waterproof bag and lashed to the side of one of the jerrycans.

One thing is clear – in a liferaft situation the rationing of water must begin immediately. Rescue, no matter how close one may be to shipping lanes, is never assured.

More than likely your body contains enough water to last you comfortably for 24 hours. After that, rationing should begin. Of course, the size of this ration depends on weather conditions, but as a general rule, a half litre a day per person should be sufficient, and when the supply begins to be depleted, this should be reduced to one-tenth of a litre per day per person.

Equally important, is the preservation of what body fluid you may already possess. Therefore, having a sunshade, remaining fully clothed, cooling your body with seawater and expending as little energy as possible are almost as vital as a source of fresh water.

When speaking about liferaft survival the question often arises: Should one drink sea water?

The British Board of Trade is quite clear on the subject. They state:

> Seafarers are reminded that if castaway they should NEVER UNDER ANY CIRCUMSTANCES DRINK SEA WATER which has not been through a distillation plant or de-salinated by chemical means. (Board of Trade, Merchant Shipping Notice No. M.500)

None the less, a number of spectacular voyages have sought to show that sea water can be drunk by castaways *in small quantities* without ill effects. Probably the most well-known advocate of this position is Dr. Alain Bombard, who in 1952 sailed across the Atlantic in a rubber dinghy.

> Everyone knows that sea water is dangerous. Consumed in large quantities it causes death by nephritis (inflammation of the kidneys) . . . I made up my mind that I would consume the permissible daily intake of salt by swallowing it in sea water. This meant that I could drink about a pint and a half of sea water a day. The chief thing I had to worry about was its effect on the Malpighian corpuscles. These form the first filter in the kidneys and have to work the hardest where there is an abnormal concentration of mineral salts. The question was how long the corpuscles could continue to work without damage. As far as I could make out, this was about five days, after which the danger of nephritis became acute.

By carefully controlling his intake, Dr. Bombard drank sea water during his voyage and survived. But it was a controlled experiment and he had a sealed reserve of fresh water in case anything went wrong.

However, no castaway knows when he will be picked up. Equally important, from the point of view of survival, is the psychological dimension. Once a castaway begins to quench his thirst from the sea, it may be difficult, if not impossible, for him to stop suddenly after four or five days, especially since at that point his thirst will be more acute.

However, another source of liquid exists – namely that which can be obtained from fish. Thor Heyerdahl, writing about the Kon-Tiki's voyage across the Pacific, points out:

> One can press the juices out by twisting pieces of fish in a cloth, or, if the fish is large, it is a fairly simple matter to cut holes in its side, which soon become filled with ooze from the fish's lymphatic glands. It does not taste good if one has anything better to drink, but the percentage of salt is so low that one's thirst is quenched.

A number of recent castaways, such as the Baileys, who floated for 117 days in the Pacific, and the Robertson family who drifted for 37 days, have also reported using the same method. On the other hand, Dr. Lindemann, who crossed the Atlantic by kyack, found he could obtain more drinkable liquid from fishes' eyes, blood and spinal fluid.

Most liferafts are equipped with very little emergency food, usually a type of vitaminized bread or biscuit sufficient for only a few days. Like an emergency water supply, a box of liferaft rations should always be ready whenever making a passage.

This can be put together quite simply, using either packaged dehydrated foods, or items such as chocolate, unsalted nuts, honey, condensed milk, peanut butter, raisins and beer in tins (which provides both food and liquid). In general tinned foods should be avoided since they often contain salt.

Another source of food is the sea itself – all one has to do is find a way to get at it.

Most castaways have complained about their lack of fishing tackle, and not simply a lack of hooks and line. What they really needed was a harpoon or spear gun. In nearly every case there were plenty of fish under or around the raft; however, they were often uninterested in whatever was on the end of the hook.

It is important to remember that in the open ocean there is little danger of eating a poisonous fish. Heart, liver, brains and roe can all be eaten; in fact, they are often more nourishing than the flesh. Although fish is highly perishable, survivors report that even in the Tropics they were able to eat fish 24 hours after catching them.

Eating our meal followed a routine. First the skins were scraped off any left-over meat and thrown over the side; next the fish heads were split in two and the small amounts of exceptionally sweet meat prised free and eaten. Sometimes we crushed the gills and found them quite palatable although it made us very thirsty. Fish livers were eaten next followed by fillets and fish eyes. (Maurice and Maralyn Bailey, *117 Days Adrift*)

Other sources of food are plankton (which can be collected with a fine net or gauze), barnacles, sea birds, turtles and seaweed.

Beyond the problem of satisfying one's basic needs in a survival situation, is the castaway's state of mind. Men have often died more quickly from panic and despair than from thirst or hunger. There is little doubt that past a certain point only a buoyant optimism, no matter how ungrounded it may be, can keep one alive. And more than that, one needs the ability to step mentally out of his situation, see it from a distance and even joke about it. Humour can often be more nourishing than a steak.

If any single civilized factor in a castaway's character helps survival, it is a well-developed sense of the ridiculous. (Dougal Robertson – *Survive the Savage Sea*)

What the Liferaft didn't Have

Here are some items castaways regretted not taking with them when they jumped into the liferaft:

A spear gun
A harpoon
Vaseline
A knife with a saw blade
Sponges
Playing cards
A heliograph
Plastic containers
Epoxy glue
Notebook and pencil
Sea anchor
Needles and thread
Gauze for straining plankton
Sailcloth for sunshade

Epilogue

If, for some reason, one or more of the recipes in this book don't turn out properly, we'd like to apologize in advance. You see, one confused night during Carnival in Brazil a gallon or so of cane juice was spilled on our notebooks and some of the writing got blurred.

We would, of course, like to hear about your experiences with this book, as we're in the process of formulating a new one – Great Culinary Disasters. Our floating address is that of our new nationality, Citizens of the Sea, where we hold passport numbers 556 and 557.

Finally, we would like to apologize to the Captains of this world. If we have been a little unkind or irreverent, this was not our intention.

We only suggest that you go to the galley, roll up your sleeves, set to work and introduce yourself to the crew. For just as *The Cook is the Captain*, the Captain should also be the Cook.

Index of Galley-Aids

Index of Recipes